NO BIG DEAL

**From Athlete to Advocate:
A Memoir of Childhood Betrayal
and a Journey to Justice**

Dear Jenny,
Thanks for being in
my tribe! This IS
a BIG DEAL!
With love,
Jenny

Endorsements

"*No Big Deal* brings you intimately inside the day-to-day world of a child navigating family life, peers, and eventually entering adolescence while being groomed and seduced by her trusted gymnastics coach. Torey illustrates clearly how so many adults make mistakes and miss the signs of a child being sexually violated because they don't know what to look for. This memoir holds promise for parents and professionals alike to protect children in the future."

Feather Berkower, LCSW, Founder of Parenting Safe Children, Child Sexual Abuse Prevention Educator & Author

"Sharing your truth is never easy, especially when you know the impact it could have on the people you care about. And yet, when you know that telling your story is critical to your own healing and the healing of millions of others, you take that risk. Which is exactly what Torey Ivanic did when she told hers. No Big Deal is a timely book that we all need to read to ensure that our children, and children everywhere, will not endure what Torey and millions of other girls and boys around the world have had to endure. Because of Torey's and other women's courage, her perpetrator went to jail for 43 years. But that level of justice is rare because most people are too afraid to confront or prosecute their perps, for fear of their safety or misplaced shame. Torey's story and her courage could be the torch that lights the way for someone else to latch onto their courage and deliver justice, while helping parents like myself learn how to make sure this never happens to our children. This is not just Torey's battle cry—it is mine and it is yours. Read this book and then give a copy to every adult you know who is willing to listen to the chorus of children's voices that need to be heard NOW."

Ursula Mentjes, Award-Winning Author of *The Belief Zone*

"Torey paints a clear picture of the sexual abuse she suffered at the hands of a trusted, respected, and loved member of the community. She describes in vivid detail her life growing up that made her vulnerable to his grooming process. Torey's story is helpful to parents, teachers, aunts, uncles, and to society in general. It helps to dispel the theory that the bad guy is scary looking, speaks loudly, or is the stranger lurking in the shadows. Instead, the monster described in Torey's case, and so many other cases, is the respected, charming, loved member of the community that parents and others trusted alike. Torey portrays a master manipulator and he would still be out there but for the courage and bravery of Torey, Samantha, and all the other women that made the most difficult step of coming forward and making sure he was held accountable. This book is a powerful reminder that we must remain vigilant in protecting children against these master manipulators and not allow an opening for the predators to gain access to any child."

Natasha (Frenchko) Natale, Former Sex Crimes Prosecutor

"On the cusp of the exposure of sexual predators and the 'Me Too' campaign, Torey's story reminds us that it's not just happening in the entertainment and political arenas. Grooming, molestation, and abuse unfold at the hands of people we are trained to readily trust: coaches, doctors, therapists, family friends, and more. As a woman whose family has been affected by sexual predators, I am deeply grateful that Torey found the courage to tell her story, put an abuser behind bars, and become an advocate for prevention. If you or a family member have a story like this, Torey's will inspire you to believe that healing is possible for you and our culture."

Amanda Johnson, Founder of True to Intention

"Torey brings us a raw and moving account of her life and the sexual abuse that changed everything. We journey alongside her as she transforms from an innocent, unsuspecting young adult to a young woman devastated by the betrayal of someone she deeply trusted. She insightfully shares the impact of this trauma on her adult relationships, until she is able to face her truth and her aggressor head-on. This is a story of vulnerability, courage, healing and redemption."

Rachel Shanken, LMHC Founder MindBodyWise

"Oprah Winfrey nailed it when she said, 'What I know for sure is that speaking your truth is the most powerful tool we all have.' Torey delivers in spades. Some truths are harder to tell and Torey does an impeccable job of sharing one tough truth. We have a long way to go in breaking the silence around sexual violence and abuse. So many have suffered in silence, drowning in a sea of shame. Many warriors have been the ones to speak up and break this silence, and Torey is one such warrior. Having survived a college rape, I suffered in silence and shame for over two decades before being able to speak my truth. Those courageous individuals who go first and bravely share their truth, unconsciously give the rest of us permission to do the same. Thank you, Torey. Thank you for the courage, the vulnerability, and the strength to share your story in a way that paves the way for so many to be able to do the same. This is the step towards healing, recovery, and freedom."

Molly Fiore, MS, Suicide Prevention Expert, Author of *Opting In*

"This is a beautifully told story of discovery, courage, and resilience. Torey's honesty regarding her own coming of age highlights shared experiences of being a woman: the difficulty understanding boundaries, the confusion of navigating complex relationships, and the empowering awareness that comes with recognizing our own value."

Stephanie Rogers, MD, MS, MPH
Assistant Professor of Medicine, University of California, San Francisco

"This is not light subject matter and not even something I'm usually brave enough to read about. Fortunately, Torey is brave enough for the both of us and No Big Deal turned into an eye-opening and rewarding journey. Torey's tenacity to not settle, to fight for her sense of self, is inspiring and I can only imagine the hope it will offer to someone currently experiencing the abuse she did. No Big Deal is a book you should read, especially if you're a young woman or a parent of one."

Greg Kuhn, Author of *Why Quantum Physicists Do Not Fail*

"Terrifying yet touching. In a society with short memory syndrome, where we move on to the next big thing once the perpetrator is caught, Torey's story addresses the residual effects and the long-term, lasting damage that can be done. In my profession, I unfortunately see similar things all too often. These damaging incidents will ripple through someone's life, wreaking havoc, affecting relationships, and tearing at the very fabric of the person's being. This book's most important message is that it CAN be overcome. *No Big Deal* is a ray of light—a beacon if you will—letting other victims know that they are not alone and that there is a path through the darkness to a better place."

Michael R Hunt, M.Ed., MPAS, PA-C

"Torey's story is one that we can all relate to. It reminds us that whether we ourselves are survivors of abuse or whether we have friends or family members who have been violated, we have all been impacted by the actions of sexual predators. Her words are raw and honest, highlighting the deep and far-reaching impacts that these acts of power and coercion have on both an individual and cultural level. However, her story is truly one of empowerment, demonstrating the change that one voice can bring about. I hope that this story will give other women to courage to come forward and speak their own truths. This book reminds us that when we say 'Me Too,' we are really saying 'Us Too.'"

Rebecca Flax, MSPAS, PA-C

"Torey first told me parts of this story around a campfire on a climbing trip in California's Sierra Nevada Mountains. It was hard for her to tell and I was moved and honored to hear it, but it's a story that must be told and one that must be heard. It's a story that must be read by survivors, young women, mothers, and the men who are part of their lives."

John Nordquist, Friend, Educator, Consultant

"A compelling narrative that takes us on a journey into the world of fifteen-year-old gymnast Torey Ivanic. We follow her from sexual trauma in her teen years to college and to adulthood, ultimately rejoicing with her when justice is served. *No Big Deal* is a must-read for anyone seeking empowerment, anyone that knows that it really is, in fact, a big deal."

Melissa Meinecke, M. Ed., Mother, Teacher, Survivor

"As someone who has experienced child sexual abuse, I was deeply moved by the authenticity, clarity, and transformative power of this book. Mrs. Ivanic highlights the insidious nature of the grooming process, and how perpetrators take advantage of a teen's desire for care and affection from a trusted adult. In this context, the tendency to misinterpret and minimize violation becomes understandable. I urge families and teens to read this, not just as memoir, but as an eye-opening, honest guide for preventing sexual violation. Ms. Ivanic is a hero in the truest sense of the word - not just for herself, but for all those impacted by sexual violation."

Lisa Foster, Founder, Parillume

"Reading Torey's book gave me more understanding on how people in positions of trust like me (a gymnastics coach) can affect lives for a long time. I commend Torey for sharing her experiences and bringing this issue into the open so that it can give hope of healing to many. I recommend this book for parents and coaches."

Stanley Chinyerere - Gymnastics Coach

"Every parent should read Torey's book *No Big Deal*. It is a really big deal to miss out on this open and raw truth telling memoir. Having experienced and survived many a 'relationshit', readers can relate and recognize the importance of honoring the boundaries we must respect for all humans. Torey writes from her heart with a tender truth."

Barbra Westfall, Parent, Educator Ally

"With the explosion of the #metoo movement, the radius of the shrapnel has touchpoints in all of our lives. As a young athlete myself, I quit my HS track team because of a local business man who stalked me while I trained for long distance on the back-country roads. No one knew that. I have never spoken about why I quit in HS, until now. Everyone respected him. Everyone liked him. But that is what predators hope for. The hope that they have enough respect in the community, power over others, and secrecy to heinously behave because young women are afraid to lose. Afraid to lose respect. Afraid to lose community support and afraid to be rejected by disbelief. *No Big Deal* has come along at a pivotal moment in our society's awareness that young women are being targeted by predators, no….they are being targeted by monsters. Torey is bringing awareness and a positive, preventative approach to a problem that has plagued our communities for way too long. Stand up and join her movement."

Carmen Trummer, Mother, Friend, Fierce Ally

"No Big Deal is a very big deal because Torey Ivanic put her courageous story to the page in a very real, vulnerable and instructive way for all audiences. Readers will gain a strong understanding of the dynamics that children, and the adults they become, face - when they experience sexual abuse in childhood. It is not the stranger who jumps out of the bushes, but a trusted person in our lives who may pose the biggest threat to children. When that happens, too often, children aren't prepared to understand what is happening, how to respond, or the impact that abuse will have on their lives - for decades. For adult survivors of childhood sexual abuse, specifically, it can be unfathomable to consider that challenges they may be currently experiencing have anything to do with something that happened so long ago, yet that is a crucial step toward healing. With very little to guide her but her own determination and the will to heal, Torey painstakingly put the pieces of a large puzzle together, lived it - and revealed it, piece by piece, so her readers could follow exactly how it was for her - each step of the way. This is an important book, and Torey is a powerful voice for truth, resilience and accountability in this #MeToo era."

Jennifer Stith, Executive Director, WINGS Foundation, Inc.

NO BIG DEAL

**From Athlete to Advocate:
A Memoir of Childhood Betrayal
and a Journey to Justice**

Torey Ivanic

By Torey Ivanic

Torey Ivanic

NO BIG DEAL

From Athlete to Advocate: A Memoir of Childhood Betrayal
and a Journey to Justice.

Torey Ivanic

Published by
Carpe Valebat LLC

www.OpenSpace4.com

Cover Design by Greg Scott

Ryan, K. (1994) *Flamingo Watching.* Copper Beach Press.

Disclaimer: The Publisher and the Author does not guarantee that anyone following
the techniques, suggestions, tips, ideas or strategies will become successful. The advice
and strategies contained herein may not be suitable for every situation. The Publisher
and Author shall have neither liability nor responsibility to anyone with respect to any
loss or damage caused, or alleged to be caused, directly or indirectly by the
information in this book. I have tried to recreate events, locales and conversations
from my memories of them. In order to maintain their anonymity in some instances I
have changed the names of individuals and places, I may have changed some
identifying characteristics and details.

ISBN: 978-1720528265

To Otis and Emi,
You are my brightest lights
and my best teachers.

To the Samantha and Torey of 1992,
You are whole, complete, and enough.
It's all going to be okay.

Table of Contents

"The final stage of healing is using what happens to you to help other people. That is healing in itself."
-*Gloria Steinem*

"Unless someone like you cares a whole awful lot, nothing is going to get better. It's not."
-*Dr. Seuss*

Foreward

Written by Rachel Shanken LMHC,
Founder MindBodyWise

I first met Torey in a six-month intensive, heart-centered professional development program where we immediately hit it off. We both recognized similar qualities in one another—our passion for wellness, our commitment to personal growth, our creative intensity, and, possibly the most foundational to our similarities, that we were both "retired" gymnasts.

Gymnasts are a very specific breed. Once you get to a certain level in gymnastics, there's nothing halfway about it. You're either all-in or you're out. Torey and I both have an all-in quality about us that made us fast friends—we immediately just "got" each other. Once the program ended, we remained in touch and continue to support each other as friends and entrepreneurs. Although we live in different parts of the country, no matter when we pick up the phone to connect, it's as if no time has passed.

When Torey wanted to share her book with me in its early stages, I was touched. I knew what this story meant to her, as she had already vulnerably shared some of the events and the deep impact they had on her life. As I've watched her navigate the writing process, I've appreciated her commitment to telling the whole truth and her hugely courageous and noble mission of creating a movement of awareness and prevention that changes the statistics. The experiences Torey went through were painful enough to endure at the time they happened, but to choose to write about them and share them takes another level of courage.

Torey's story provides survivors of sexual trauma both validation for feeling what they feel and hope that they can heal. And for those who haven't been through similar experiences, her book is a warning and a guide—a way of learning what to look out for and how to aim to prevent it from happening to themselves and their children.

And the timing couldn't be more perfect. Our society needs this book.

With the #MeToo movement, there are many people speaking out about unwanted sexual experiences, but very few of them have shared the full landscape of who they were before and after the abuse. We rarely hear about how the crimes they underwent have impacted their relationships with others and most importantly their relationships with themselves. Torey shares beyond the scope of the abuse itself. She insightfully lets us in on her vulnerabilities prior to the abuse, as well as how the abuse changed her life thereafter. Our world needs the whole story, so we can start to take preventative action and stop blaming the survivors.

As a Licensed Mental Health Counselor and MindBodyWise (body-integrated) therapist specializing in trauma-recovery over the past ten years, I was honored when Torey asked me to share some therapeutic recommendations for navigating your journey through these pages.

As you read *No Big Deal,* you may notice uncomfortable feelings emerging for you. This is completely normal. Whether you're a survivor of sexual abuse or not, you are human, and empathy is a natural part of being human. Simply put: it's painful to read about painful things.

It's important that as you read, you pay attention to your feelings and the body sensations that arise for you. Stay tuned into yourself. Even though you might want to avoid feeling those uncomfortable feelings, checking out doesn't circumvent the discomfort forever. In fact, what you resist will persist and your feelings will find their way to you later, when you least expect them.

I recommend that you pause between chapters, take a breath, and notice what's going on inside you before moving forward with the next chapter. It only takes a moment to check in with yourself and it can provide a lot of information about how you're responding to the material.

If you notice mild feelings and/or mild body sensations arising, consider taking a break from reading to do some self-care. Self-care preferences are different for everyone, but consider the following options: take a walk, close your eyes and breathe quietly for a minute or two, call a friend, go to a yoga class or do an online yoga class, take a bath, or listen to calming music.

If you notice intense feelings, flashbacks, and/or strong body sensations (fast heartbeat, labored breathing, weakness in your limbs, going numb, freezing up, difficulty with vision, or extreme tension), close the book if you haven't already.

Also, keep awareness turned on, even when you aren't actively reading the book. Nightmares, increased fear or worry, agitation, crying out of the blue, increased anxiety, or acting out in anger are signs that your body, mind, and heart are responding to the material in the book even when you aren't actively reading it. Your subconscious is processing the material and sending warning signals to you in its own unique way. Your body is asking you to listen and to take heed.

The tricky thing about trauma is that it can be triggered when you least expect it and the more you try to ignore it, the worse it gets. Also, the longer you let it continue without getting support, the harder it becomes to navigate. I recommend that if you experience any of the symptoms mentioned above, consider doing some self-care and don't wait to get professional help.

With the help of someone who specializes in trauma and the body, you can absolutely and positively heal. Because trauma is a whole-body experience, look for someone trained in one or more of the following: yoga therapy with a mental health license, sensorimotor psychotherapy, somatic psychotherapy, Gestalt therapy, EEG Biofeedback, and/or a therapist who is certified in EMDR.

A few more words about trauma…

It's vital to know that no matter what happened, the trauma you experienced wasn't your fault, nor was it in your control to manage your response to the trauma while it was happening. Neuroscience has proven that the logic and language centers of your brain shut off when you're in a traumatic situation. Thus, during a traumatic event, you respond from your body. The memory of the experience is imprinted in mixed-up visual flashes in your brain and sensations in your body. You have zero control over this automatic process.

Neuroscience has also proven that your body "remembers" painful experiences even when your mind forgets them. This means that you can't *think* your way out of trauma. It also means that a memory of a traumatic experience that you had forgotten may emerge long after it happens. In order to heal, you need to work with your body in connection with your mind.

Finally, even if you don't have trauma in your history (or you don't think you do), there is such a thing as vicarious trauma. By witnessing or hearing accounts of traumatic events, you can become traumatized. This is more common with persistent exposure to accounts of trauma (i.e. psychotherapists, ER doctors, service men and women, etc.), but it can happen with less exposure as well.

While reading, aim to stay attuned to your feelings and body sensations. Don't ignore them. Persistently intense feelings don't go away without being addressed. For some time, compartmentalizing your feelings might work, but eventually your feelings will arise repeatedly and with more intensity until you give some attention to your mental health. Unresolved feelings often arise as depression or anxiety or even panic attacks.

As you read *No Big Deal*, my hope is that you get informed on multiple levels. My wish is that Torey's story about the insidious ways that sexual predators can sneak their way into the lives of even the most intelligent, motivated, and self-aware people will raise your antennae so that you can prevent abuse like this from happening to you and your loved ones.

Additionally, I hope that you use this book to get informed about yourself. Can you give yourself the space to pause and feel what you feel? Can you stay in tune with yourself, even when the feelings are uncomfortable? Can you honor the signals (and warning signs) of your body? Will you take care of yourself in the ways that you need to heal and grow? Can you ask for help when you need it?

The most important thing to remember is that healing is always possible. It starts with paying attention to the signs, knowing you don't have to do it alone, and loving yourself enough to take the first step.

Rachel Shanken, LMHC

www.mindbodywise.com

Prologue

Spring 2006

As I sat at my desk and finished typing the note on my last patient, I could feel the tears welling up again. My left ring finger was empty, and so was my heart. I couldn't believe my tear ducts had anything left but I couldn't hold it back. Here they came again.

What is wrong with me? Why can't I get this right? And if it DOES have anything to do with Greg, I wonder if Samantha is dealing with the same relationshit? Maybe she's over it?

I opened my email and started a new message:

```
From: Torey V.
To: Samantha
Subject: hello Samantha!
Date: Thu, 25 May 2006 11:39:44 -0700


Hey--
How are ya? I've been thinking about you a
lot-- probably for a lot of reasons, and
just wanted to catch up and see where you
were and what you were up to...
I'm in Cali working as a PA in a small town
called Three Rivers. Life is pretty good all
in all. I have a house and a dog and I love
my job most days...
HOW ARE YOU?
```

```
thinking of you,
torey
```

I winced as I read it before hitting SEND, wondering if it was too short.

Screw it, I have to start somewhere. Maybe Samantha has the answers.

I hit SEND, wiped my eyes, and wished the nauseated feeling in my stomach would go away.

I called it off. I gave the ring back. I'm about to turn thirty and I am single...AGAIN.

I flipped through the charts on my desk.

It's so hard to listen to people talk about their annoying rashes or foot pain when I just called off my freaking marriage. I've broken up with MANY, MANY guys in my life, but never have I been physically ill from it.

I had picked up my pen and the chart for the next patient and begun walking toward the door when it hit me: *This isn't about him, is it? This is about ME.*

I walked back out to the lobby, chart in hand, and called back my next patient. I'd known her for several years and she could tell I had been crying.

"Are you okay?" she asked.

"Not really, but it will get better. How can I help you today?" I mustered with a gentle smile.

I took care of her med refills, gave her some thoughts on why her weight still wasn't coming off, and sent her on her way. Before she left, she hugged me and told me it would be okay.

God, I hope she's right.

I went back to my computer and checked my email. Samantha had written back!

```
To: Torey V.
From: Samantha
Hi Torey!
```

Good to hear from you. Life is pretty good
for me, similar to you it
sounds. I coach track at Bowling Green, like
it most days, have a house and a chocolate
lab. Been thinking about you as well, just
not too good at keeping in touch. Always
keep myself a little too busy.

Samantha

I blinked my eyes as a million questions and possibilities
flooded my mind.

*Interesting, she doesn't mention a husband or even a
boyfriend. I'm going for it.*

I opened another email:

From: Torey V.
To: Samantha
Subject: Re: hello Samantha!

Glad to hear back from you. What's your
dog's name? My dog is my child. His name is
Brutus and I spoil the hell out of him.
    I'm kind of in a self-analysis place
'cause I just broke off an engagement and I
guess I'm looking back and thinking maybe I
didn't deal with all the shit that I needed
to get over from my past. It always made me
sad that you and I didn't stay close but for
some reasons that might have been good for
us too. If you don't want to talk about any
of this just let me know-- but I'm wondering
if you ever saw a therapist for any extended
period of time? I just started and I haven't
even gotten into anything with him yet--
mostly just talking about my relationship

with my ex-fiancé Justin. I've read a couple books on divorce and how that can play into our lives... it's been sort of interesting. Things I never would have thought of. I really think my parents' divorce has made me a much more independent woman in some ways, but also added to my lack of trust in people and men especially. Then there was the whole Greg thing... I can only imagine if this stuff affects me at all, it might still affect you even more. I hope that's not the case and you are a well-adjusted happy adult :). Sometimes I think I can appear that way but on the inside, I'm a freaking mess. Who knows, everyone has their stuff, right?

Anyway, I don't mean to dump this on you or bring up shitty memories. I think you and I had a lot more good times than bad. I hope maybe we can be better at staying in touch and maybe even see each other sometime if I ever come back to Ohio. Anyway, if you want to keep talking about any of this I'd love to hear your thoughts. Like I said, big life change lately is making me question my sanity... I'll get over it.

I really do hope you are well.

torey
559-XXX-XXXX

Whew. I did it. I feel a little better. At least I took a step. I have an appointment with my therapist in two more days. I can make it two more days, right?

26

I nodded affirmatively with sheer determination, went back out to the front desk, and dropped off the charts I had finished. I checked to see if there were any other patients on the schedule for that morning and was heading back to my office for my lunch break, when my cell phone rang.

It was a number I didn't recognize, but I answered: "Hello, this is Torey."

"Hi, it's Samantha."

My heart skipped a beat, and my breathing quickened. *I can't believe she's calling!*

"Hello! I'm so glad you called. I was just going to lunch, so I have an hour. Do you have some time?" I asked with a touch of hesitation.

"I do. I'm not sure we can catch up on twelve years in an hour, but let's try." I could hear the smile in her voice and see her sparkly green eyes, ivory Irish skin, and flowing brown hair in my mind's eye.

Wow. It's so good to hear her voice.

We took turns sharing about what we had done, where we had lived, and guys we had dated. Though we didn't catch up on everything, we both very clearly saw a common thread. We both had a ton of relationshit.

Samantha had just broken up with a boyfriend and she could totally relate to my frustration with dating and feeling like a failure. I told her I had started looking back and I was seriously wondering if what happened with Greg had affected me more than I would have ever liked to admit. I shared how working as a Physician Assistant, I had heard a lot of stories of sexual violation and saw the long-term effects of those traumas on my patient's sense of self-worth, their ability to trust, and their long-term happiness. And…if I was honest, whenever I listened to their stories, I felt like I was looking in a mirror on some level. Yet, what happened to me was no big deal compared to what happened to her and many others. I confided that I didn't want to live like this anymore. I wanted more than just a house, a dog, and a good job. I wanted a husband and a family, and I wanted to be truly happy, not constantly searching for more. I was content, but never satisfied because I knew there was something missing.

That conversation not only reconnected me to a long-lost friend, it started us both down a path neither of us could have imagined taking, and probably could not have braved alone. Two years later, the man who had betrayed and deceived us was sent to prison for forty-three years, and we stepped into an open space where we now have loving husbands, beautiful children, and a freedom we never knew was possible.

And now, it's time for all of us to open space for truth, healing, justice, and, most importantly, prevention.

I was sexually violated by my gymnastics coach at the age of fifteen and, on the surface, you may never have known, because I kept telling myself it wasn't a big deal. You may be walking around your "successful" life with a story just like mine, or maybe someone you love is, and you may not even know it.

This is my story of betrayal and pain, as well as courage, strength, resilience, honesty, gratitude, and justice. Until I owned my own truth, that what I had thought was no big deal was actually a criminal act, my train was on a broken set of tracks. When I finally spoke my truth, I took back the power of how my story would end...and let me tell you, it *is* possible to heal, to enjoy a loving relationship, to have your own family. I know it's possible, because I'm living it.

And, if I'm honest, as I go back through the moments of the story you are about to read, I find I'm still more comfortable passing over details and superficially addressing key moments because let's face it—it's not easy to write, read, or talk about sexual violation.

It's not easy to talk about the fact that someone I loved and trusted took advantage of me. It's not easy to share the inappropriate confiding and touching. It's not easy to discuss the messiness that confusion and pain created in my life, especially when I spent the greater part of my life trying to erase it from my memory and live like it never happened.

In fact, it's so difficult to have these conversations that I just avoided them, until I couldn't anymore—that moment when I called off an engagement and felt like a completely broken human.

I worked hard to heal and put the story behind me until I learned that the man who had taken advantage of me had moved back to our hometown and was seeing young gymnasts as patients. My stomach clenched with fear.

Not on my watch.

It's sad, but it's true—our society isn't safe. Statistics show that 700,000 registered sex offenders live among us, but that is the tip of the iceberg when it comes to the number of predators who haven't been called out yet. Those without a prior conviction are often dressed in leaders', coaches', and experts' clothing. One in three girls and one in six boys have a story just like this, or worse, by the age of 18. BY THE AGE OF 18! This is a BIG DEAL.

The only way to change our society is for us to stop trying to put the stories behind us and speak up, address it, and open space for a new normal.

Healing doesn't have to come in the form of torturous conversations in a therapist's office, reliving the nightmare of it time and again, or drugs you take for the rest of your life. There are hundreds of fun and adventurous ways to discover the way and the space in which to heal, and if you have healing to do, you probably already have a tool kit of your own.

When I started writing this book, I thought my goal was to help others see what an impact sexual violation may have on their life and help them take a step toward healing. By the end of the book, I knew that I wanted to think bigger and make a movement to change our societal views on this topic. I want to help PREVENT the crimes in the first place. My hope is that your first step toward changing our society and preventing more victims will be simply joining the Open Space movement that says, "It IS a Big Deal!"

I'm asking you to join me on this adventure to make our world a better place, first and most simply, by reading my story (hang in there, it has a happy ending). If you choose to become a part of the Open Space community to stand with me and create a safer future for our children, or you want to share your story and own your truth, or you want to take that huge step and report a crime against you, fantastic! I hope I can be a source of inspiration and even support to you.

If you hold this book in your hand, you hold an opportunity to see things from a different perspective. You can quietly or loudly confront a part of our society that is stealing our safety as well as a sacred part of many of our friends and loved ones.

If you have a similar story, please take some time and the space to own your truth and allow healing to start. No matter what happened to you, whether it was verbal, physical, brutal, gentle, "consensual", enjoyable, or terrifying—if there's a part of you that wonders whether or not it was right, it probably wasn't.

If you are a supporter, give your loved one the space to share with you and the support and strength to own their truth and explain to you why it really is a big deal. Hear them, hold them, love them.

If you want to bring up the next generation so those dreadful statistics are different, let's open space to empower kids to know they are in control of their bodies and they can say "No" with confidence.

Let's address this topic the way it needs to be addressed, and not the way that's comfortable and easy. Let's be proud to say that sexual predators are not welcome in our schools or churches or gymnasiums. Betraying and violating youth is a BIG DEAL. Let's find the open space to treat it like one.

Chapter One:
Daydreaming in Dandelions

Spring 1987

I laid back in the grass and stared up into a rare blue-sky day in Ohio. Heat radiated from the ground, but I was a little chilly from the breeze on my slightly sweaty skin. The wind through the trees sounded magical and promised a few more blue-sky days before Ohio became grey again. I could smell the buttery acidity from the dandelions all around me. I had been playing for the past two hours with my neighbor friend, but she had to go home. On my way, running back from her house, I had stopped to just *lay there* in the wide-open space of the Kent State Branch lawn. This time of year was my favorite because Kent didn't believe in Chemlawn and their entire green space was *covered* in huge yellow dandelions. I'd been told as a child they were technically weeds, but to me they were beautiful. I loved how fluffy and joyful and plentiful they were. It was like the earth was smiling back at me. I knew I had gymnastics practice in just an hour or so and probably needed to get home, but I just wanted to feel the freedom of lying there for a few more minutes.

No schedule, no commitments, no brother, no mom, no dad, no dog—just me, in nature.

I was happy.

I hustled home, threw my favorite splatter paint leotard and shorts on my strong ten-year-old body, and grabbed a banana and a peanut butter and jelly sandwich to eat in the van. Practices on Saturdays were from 1 p.m. – 4 p.m., but we left at 11:30 a.m. so I had plenty of time before practice to do extra work.

I'd been doing gymnastics for almost eight years already. It was a huge part of my life, and Mom was almost always the one to take me to practice.

Mom was beautiful and young (for almost forty). Her big blondish-brown 80's curls framed her gentle, round face and kind eyes that lit up when she gave her amazing hugs. She was loving and sweet and always taking care of my brother and me. She worked part-time teaching Home Economics, so she was there when we got home from school. She swam in the pool with us in the summers and she picked up frogs, toads, and even snakes to show us and teach us about the wildlife in our midst. She wasn't afraid. She'd been a Girl Scout and always seemed to know the names of all the trees and flowers. At thirty-nine years old, she was in really good shape. She had never been an athlete before she had kids, but she started "jogging" after I was born and found she was good at it. She won a lot of trophies in the 10K races she ran nearby and was almost always faster than fifty minutes. Fit, social, and always smiling, it's no wonder everyone loved my mom.

On my way to the car, I saw Dad and my brother, Derek, out in the garage refinishing a piece of furniture for a Boy Scout project. I poked my head in the garage to say goodbye.

Derek was only two years older than me, but a lot bigger. His brown hair had sawdust in it, flaking off onto his cut-off Camo shorts and United Local t-shirt. He wasn't as athletic as I was, but he was strong and competent at many things. He got good grades, had lots of good friends, built things, mowed the lawn, was generally much cooler than me, and was never without a snide comment about why I was useless or stupid. I loved my big brother, but he wasn't easy to live with.

Derek had a rag with wood stain on it in his hand. He had been busy all morning sanding the piece and now he was on to the stain. He was a hard worker, and it always seemed like he was up to some type of project. He and Dad often worked all weekend on things around the house and the lawn. Derek was ALWAYS his helper. It may never have been said, but I felt like, because I was a girl, I didn't get to be Dad's helper.

Girls don't use power tools? Girls can't build things?

Then there was my Dad, with his blonde comb-over and his mustache, leaning against the wall of the garage, smoking a White Owl, and giving Derek some "constructive" criticism. His five-foot eleven-inch, fairly thin frame was shirtless and tan from all the hours he spent working in the yard or doing construction and touted a small 6-pack of beer belly. He was wearing his glasses and I saw the hanky in his back pocket that he always kept handy to clean them with, or to lend me to blow my nose.

"Bye, guys!" I ran through the garage, out into the driveway, and jumped into the van.

The first half of the 45-minute drive to the gym rambled through rolling rural Ohio farmland, then entered a more suburban area where the gym was located. Dionne Warwick and Lionel Richie played on the radio and Mom and I sat in comfortable silence on the drive. When she dropped me off, I pranced up the wide brown steps to the second floor to find my friends and play for a while before practice.

It was getting hot already, even though it was only spring. That's what happens in a metal-roofed, two-story building in the humid Midwest. It gets drippy hot.

I stood at the main door and scanned the gym.

There they are! I found my two best friends- Danielle with her blonde curly hair, strong hugs, and body that almost mirrored mine; and Tracy, taller with naturally curly brown hair, deep brown eyes, and a soft gentle face.

I dropped off my t-shirt at my locker, we exchanged exuberant hugs, and then the three of us worked on double backs from a springboard to the pit. We'd launch ourselves into the air and flip just a little more than one time and land on our backs. We were nowhere close to learning that skill, but we loved trying. Fifteen minutes before practice started, we went to the trampolines for some "real" playtime. We tried to see who could do the most back tucks in a row before they got dizzy, lost their balance, or fell off the tramp. Danielle and Tracy were both a little better than me at gymnastics, but it was still a fun game.

Carole and Terri, our coaches, called us to the floor and practice began. We did some laps, running and skipping the perimeter of the floor, and then lined up to begin our floor workout. Practices on Saturdays were long enough that we usually got to all four events: bars, beam, floor, and vault. It was spring and the competitive season was over, so we were mainly working on skills and not routines. I loved pushing myself to see what skills I could get next. I really wanted to do a standing back tuck on beam. *That would be awesome.*

It was a pretty typical day at the gym, and I left tired as usual.

Sunny days were the BEST for napping on the way home, and typically I woke up as I felt the van pull into our gravel driveway. For some reason, this day was different. I didn't feel the right-hand turn or hear the gravel under the tires before the engine shut off. I woke up, and Mom and I were in the Kmart parking lot in Salem.

I didn't know we were stopping to buy anything, I thought as I took in my surroundings.

"Honey, we need to talk," my mom started, with a slightly furrowed brow. "Let's hop in the back," she nodded toward the back of our tan 1980 Dodge caravan.

I suddenly felt a pit in my stomach as I crawled through to the bench seat in the back. *Why do we need to talk in the backseat while sitting in the Kmart parking lot? This is weird. Whatever it is, it must be a big deal.*

She didn't beat around the bush. She just said it, straight up, "Your dad and I are getting divorced." Her eyes were a little misty, but her voice was matter-of-fact.

My heart broke and my throat constricted, forcing water to pour from my eyes. I collapsed into her arms.

What.................the....................? Seriously? I had NO IDEA there was a problem. How is this possible? We have an amazing life. Sure, Derek and I fight like cats and dogs and gymnastics costs a lot, but I thought we were happy? How is this happening?

I'm not sure how long Mom let me sit there in a puddle of tears, but eventually she got into the driver's seat and took me to my Grandma's house. I walked up the couple of steps to the sliding door and pulled it hard to open it, not bothering to close it since Mom was behind me. I walked into the kitchen where my sweet little Grandma caught me in her arms and gave me a loving hug. I couldn't collapse into her like I wanted to, because at ten years old, I was almost as big as her, and she seemed fragile from her emphysema.

"Go get some cookies and something to drink, Honey," she said with a smile. "Everything will be okay."

Walking to the fridge, I was surprised to see Derek sitting at the kitchen table, eating cookies and playing solitaire like it was just an average day at Grandma's.

Why isn't he crying? What's wrong with him? Does he not know that our world just blew up?

Grandma and Mom went back outside to talk, and I found myself alone with Derek.

I was still tearful, but I managed to choke out, "How long have you known that they are getting divorced?"

"Not long, but DUH, it just makes sense. They're always fighting," he responded nonchalantly.

What fighting? What is he even talking about? Ugh, why does he always know more than me and seem to "get" life in a way I don't? I can't take this.

I couldn't sit there at the table, where we usually ate cookies and played gin rummy or Acey Duecy, laughing and having fun.

I can't sit in this happy and good place and feel like this. This is a big deal for me, and I can't pretend it's not.

I took my plate of cookies and sat in Grampa's chair, turned on the TV, and the tears started rolling down my cheeks again.

I want to run away. How's the world going to work now? Where am I going to live? Am I going to have to quit gymnastics?

35

This is the worst day of my life.

Chapter Two:
Sharing in a Shower Stall

Spring 1987

No one scheduled me a therapy appointment, but I somehow created my own. It was in the women's bathroom at the gym. Specifically, it was in the shower stall and my therapist was either Tracy or Danielle (or both), my two most trusted girlfriends. What amazing friends they were to listen to me cry, and talk about all the turmoil in my household. Unlike my brother, they seemed to see this as quite a big deal, and if empathy were dollars, those two would have been millionaires. I can't imagine how many hours they spent counseling me on that wood-slatted bench next to the brown and orange shag carpeted bathroom floor.

"What's the latest?" Tracy asked.

"We went to a family wedding last weekend, and as Mom and Derek and I were leaving, Dad was running after us, and he must have been upset, because he tripped and fell and broke his glasses. His face was bleeding a little. It was late, and he and Mom were both upset. I just climbed in the van and closed the door, but it was scary." I almost managed to get it all out without choking up, but the tears were already rolling. Danielle leaned over and put her arm around me as I sucked in a huge sob.

"I feel like I just cry all the time now. I sometimes climb up on the roof outside my room with a book and just read for hours. I don't know how to just be there anymore, knowing Mom and I are

37

moving out soon."

"When are you moving? And where are you moving to?" Danielle asked with a tilt of her blonde-haired head.

"Mom and I are moving right after school is out, so two more weeks. Derek is staying with Dad. Derek and I were fighting yesterday and I went to my room crying and Mom stuck her head in and all she said was 'only two more weeks.' It's like she thinks it's good and I am looking forward to it. I've never lived in another house. I can't take my pets. It all just makes me sick."

When I just couldn't look in their eyes anymore, my gaze drifted to the dingy off-white shower curtain with the spots of black mold creeping up from the bottom. Funky bathroom smells wafted in on us, a toilet occasionally flushed, while my tears just kept falling. From the day that my Mom told me of the divorce, it seemed like a constant battle in our house. What I thought was a perfect and happy household, was suddenly NOT.

What happened? Why is MY family divorcing? Is there something I could do? If I quit gymnastics, would it be better? Gymnastics is so expensive, and it's always a source of stress and conflict. Is this my fault?

I don't remember any words of wisdom or gems of truth coming from either of my friends, but that wasn't why they were in that stall. They weren't going to stop my parent's divorce and neither was I, but that was the first time in my life that I experienced the incredible power of someone sitting with me, allowing me to feel, and validating my feelings. They were the best ten-year-old therapists that I could have had.

Five minutes before practice started, I wiped my eyes and we launched ourselves out into the gym – that playground where little pixie girls did amazingly strong and athletic tricks for hours and hours. Yes, we had "man hands" with bloody, callused, bar-beaten palms. And yes, we had more muscle definition than a lot of college athletes, but we were still cute little girls bounding around, flipping upside down, swinging like monkeys, and mostly smiling. The gym was my playground, and I found solace in the consistency of that place, those people, and the ability to lose myself in physical movement.

The gym was big, three tennis courts big, to be exact. That's what it had been before they turned it into a gymnastics center. It had high ceilings and lots of space that held two full floor exercise mats (40ft x 40ft), four sets of uneven parallel bars, two vaults, about ten beams, two sets of parallel bars, one set of rings, two high bars, two full-sized trampolines with a platform between them, and a large pre-school area. Separating the front of the gym and front floor from the back was a large platform that led to an above ground pit. There were lockers and offices upstairs as well as a small area where parents could sit and watch. On the way out, near the steps, there were the restrooms and a small area with couches, a TV, and vending machines.

Above the couch a window looked down into a racket ball court on the first floor. This often became our perch as we waited for our friends to get their drinks or finish in the bathroom. Next to the racquetball court downstairs was an old men's locker room that wasn't used much anymore, and a tanning room that could be accessed from the hall or the men's locker room. There was also a large aerobics room on the opposite side of the racquetball courts where we sometimes did our conditioning, because it was air conditioned, and so much cooler down there.

The gym seemed to have a life of its own. With the teams present, the radio playing, the chalk filling the air, and a huge amount of energy being exerted, it was if the gym itself was breathing. There could be forty or fifty team kids in there, plus another fifty class kids at one time. There was a lot of movement, noise, and energy. At the end of the night, when everyone had left, and I heard the crackle of the fluorescent lights being turned off, it seemed like a huge sleeping giant. Wide open, almost as if you were outside at night.

In that space, I could somehow separate from the pain and sadness that I felt while talking about the divorce with Tracy and Danielle. I kept it in the stall most of the time, but I had planted a deep dark seed of pain in a small corner of my happy fun place. It would come back in now and then, but I always had to get out of

my mind and into my body to do the next event. Gymnastics was
hard work, and there's no way I could be daydreaming or caught
up in my own thoughts and still nail a beam routine. It required not
just strength and flexibility, but serious mental focus. Skills were
repeated hundreds or thousands of times before they were perfect
enough for competition.

In the spring of 1987, I was a Class III, which meant I didn't
do anything too difficult or scary yet. I was working my way to
Class III Optional, the coveted level where you didn't have to do
routines that everyone else did, and could pick your own floor
music. That song from the nineteen eighties Class III floor routine
will forever be ingrained in my brain. *Ugh. Duh nan ah nan uh,
duh nan ah nan nuh, duh nan duh nan duhnt duhnt, duhnt!*

Carole and Terri were my coaches and they were like a
delicate Tweedle Dee and Tweedle Dum (in a good way). They
always had perfectly white Reeboks, matching uniforms, and an air
of precision and grace. They were well-manicured, if you will.
Actually, Terri and Carole were like really nice aunts, sweet to us,
rewarding us with Hershey's kisses when we got our skills. They
weren't overly strict or focused on perfection, and seemed to be
there for the love of the sport and because they wanted us to have
fun. They taught us not only gymnastics, but about how to treat
one another and how to work hard. They made us feel safe and
loved.

Greg Dew was the coach of the higher levels and he was
larger than life, about the size of Terri plus Carole and then maybe
a medium-sized dog. He was a body builder and at least three
times the size of any of us gymnasts. Dressed in his uniform, a
polo shirt and shorts, he was always a bit sweatier and goofier than
Terri or Carole. Greg was loud, charismatic, and always seemed to
be happy. He was attending the local university, studying his pre-
requisites for chiropractic college, but he somehow found his way
into coaching gymnastics. Though he had never been a gymnast,
he was strong, necessary at the level of gymnastics he was
coaching, as he had to lift the gymnasts and catch them a lot. He
was the coach and always the main spotter for the higher-level

girls, but Terri and Carole still helped us with the dance moves and fine-tuning that made up a good routine.

Greg would spot Tracy and I on double backs off the springboard and onto a pit, years before we were close to perfecting that skill. He basically just threw us in the air and we held on for two rotations. Terri and Carole might not have been able to spot us when we got to weigh ninety pounds, as they barely weighed more than that themselves.

Greg was a presence in the gym and it was hard not to notice him when you walked in off the street. He had impeccable posture and he was just really big. Plus, he was fun. He had a lot of games that he played with the all the kids at the gym, not just the team. For example, he had us tuck up into a little ball and held us in the palm of one hand above his head. Other times, he would have us lay flat in his arms with a super tight body and he would throw us in the air and see how many rotations we could spin our body before he caught us. He also would start at one end of the floor exercise area, on his hands and knees, and begin crawling across to the other side. Our goal (all ten or more of us at the same time) was to stop him, by crawling all over him and pulling him back to slow him down. Greg was very religious and made it well known that he didn't drink or swear or do anything bad. He talked a lot about his faith, but not really about God. To me, it came across that he was almost holy.

I can't wait to get on Greg's team, I thought.

Today, even though I was still just a Class III, I was working on my standing back tuck. I was good at them and Carole thought I could take it to the beam.

I stood with my arms above my head and my body tight, my right foot tucked into the arch of my left. I stretched up, then swung my arms down quickly, and back up while I jumped at the same time and flipped my little self around. Boom. Stick. I landed it with my feet tight together, right on the line on the floor. I raised my hands up and out in the shape of a "V" with my "pretty hands" to finish. "Pretty hands" always kind of cracked me up because I was such a tomboy, but I basically just dropped my middle finger

41

down a bit and stretched my other fingers out straight.

"Nice, T," Carole smiled.

I did it again, and again, and again.

"Time to take it to the low beam?" she asked, one eyebrow up in a small challenge.

I smiled back at her and nodded. Four inches wide, sixteen feet long, but this low beam was only about six inches high.

Not a big deal if I miss it.

I stood there, wiggled my feet into place, raised my arms up, and then FLIP, and stick. I nailed it. I did three, and then fell off on one. It wasn't a bad fall though.

"You got this, T," Greg encouraged from where he was coaching bars.

"Yeah, Torey, you do," Danielle said.

She was next to me working on her back handspring.

I did three more and stuck all three.

"You ready to take it to the medium?" Carole asked, her sparkling eyes telling me she believed in me.

I took a deep breath and said, "Yeah, you think I'm ready? I want three more sticks down here first." I started again, feet in place, wiggle, arms up, breathe, go! Flip, stick.

Nice, I thought. *I've got this. A year ago, I never would have thought I'd be doing this.*

I did two more and I knew it was time to move it up. The "medium" beam was about two feet off the ground. Still not too big of a deal even if I accidentally straddled the beam.

Carole saw me step up to the medium beam and asked, "Do you want a spot?"

I thought about it for a second, but I was feeling so good, I shook my head at her. "I've got it."

Back tuck, stick. Back tuck, stick. Back tuck, stick. I did ten before I even knew it. I was ready to take it higher.

I didn't think I'd be doing this today. Wow. I've got this. It really feels good, like I am strong and big and can do anything.

"Carole, I'm going to take it to the high beam," I said with a smile.

"Yeah, okay, you've got this, T! Do you want a spot on the high beam?"

"Maybe just stand next to me?" I asked. The girls on my team were all paying attention now. I had been working on this skill for a few weeks but had yet to do it on the high beam.

I hopped up onto the four-foot-high, four-inch-wide, sixteen-foot-long, leather coated Spieth Anderson beam, and got my positioning. Carole stood next to me but didn't put her hand up on my back. She was there as much for moral support as anything. I stood there staring down at my feet, interlaced perfectly. My little toes were just off the edge on each side. I raised my arms. *I just did ten of these on the medium beam, this is no different. I've got this. No big deal, Torey, go for it.* I wiggled, I breathed, I raised my hands, back tuck, stick! I finished with my arms up and a huge smile.

There was applause from my teammates and a hug from Carole, but what surprised me was Greg. He walked over from his team on bars and said, "Nice work, T! I think you earned a Jolly Rancher!" and gave me a high five.

"Thanks," I said with an embarrassed smile and asked Carole if I could go get a drink.

I walked out to the drinking fountain feeling really good. *I already have a skill for my optional routine. This is cool! Greg even watched me and gave me a high five! I'm going to move up sooner than I thought.*

Back home that night, the realization that we only had two weeks before my family physically separated hit me hard. I laid in my bed looking out at the dark night and the pine trees outside my window, thinking about what it would be like to have a new room, a new yard, and a new school. Tears started coming as fear bubbled up inside me, but then I thought back to my standing back tuck on the high beam and my brain swam in contentment and satisfaction.

I did it. Gymnastics is my life. I love it so much. I'm getting pretty good. I'm so glad that we are moving closer to the gym and Mom promised me I wouldn't have to quit. Derek will still have his friends and his scout troop and maybe it will all be okay like Grandma said. It'll be weird not to have Derek around. It'll be weird to be so far away from all my friends from school.

Derek and I never really questioned the decision our parents made to split us up. Mom told me it was because Derek might have a harder time changing schools than I would, which made absolutely no sense to me because I always felt like he was the more confident and grounded kid. I was shy and scared all the time and terrified to leave what I knew, on so many levels. Now, the only constant would be the gym.

Chapter Three:
Puzzled on the Platform

Fall 1989

Three years later, I was riding to the gym with Bob, my stepdad. He was a short, red-headed lawyer who my mom had dated for several years in high school before she dated my dad. I thought back to meeting him outside our garden-level apartment in 1988, the year it had been just Mom and me.

That year was pretty good. I wish it had just been the two of us for longer.

My friend Lilly had lived in the same apartment complex, and I had known her since I was little. Our moms had gone to high school together and her parents had divorced before mine. I had a new room and an immediate best friend whose house was a short bike ride away. Lilly was a year older than me, tall and thin with the classic eighties perm (we all had them). She was sweet and funny, and we laughed a lot. I was as comfortable walking into her house as I was my own and I loved her like a sister. She got the whole divorce thing, and though we didn't have too many deep talks, she was just there to hang out, laugh, and play with. I don't even know how many times we watched *Ferris Buehler* that year. Unfortunately, after just over a year at the apartment and a rough year at a new school, my mom introduced me to Bob and, after what seemed like just a couple months, I was standing at their wedding. We moved into a house with him in the fall of my seventh-grade year, and Lilly and I weren't as close geographically after that, making it harder to keep our friendship strong.

Seventh grade went okay. I had a bigger bedroom at the house, but I felt uncomfortable living with Bob. He had been married once before for a few years but had mostly lived alone and didn't have any experience with kids. He ate annoyingly fast and made me feel like I lived in his house, not mine. I didn't know how to talk to him and it seemed like I had always done something wrong. I was still visiting Derek and Dad almost every other weekend, and that felt less and less like home too. They both thought I should go back and live with them, and they weren't afraid to share that fact. I felt guilty and torn all the time. It had been more than a year of living with Bob and this school year was proving seriously challenging.

I don't know what my problem is. I can't stop crying at school. Lilly is in high school now. Maybe that's it, but come on, I am thirteen years old and I have other friends. What is wrong with me? It totally sucks that that hot guy Matt sits in front of me every day while I cry too. Jesus, I am a mess.

Bob turned right onto the main road where the gym was located and snapped me out of my spiral of thoughts. He turned down the radio and asked, "What time is practice over again?"

I shook my head a bit and answered, "Nine," as he turned right into the gym driveway. It was just after five o'clock so I had almost a full hour before practice officially started. He pulled to the corner of the lot near the door, and I climbed out of his little red sports car and said a quick "Thanks" without a smile.

Whew. It's good to be at the gym. I rarely ever cry at the gym anymore. This is where I know who I am and that I am good at something. I ran up the steps and got ready for practice. *I just want to be alone and work on my beam routine.* I went to the back floor and found a line. I went through my beam routine again and again. As I did, my mind drifted to Matt in my English class. *He must think I'm a total basket case. Why can't I stop crying every day in school?*

After four passes of my beam routine, Danielle showed up. I

saw her coming in and met her at the locker to give her a hug. We went back to the trampolines for some fun before "real" practice. We were both on Greg's team and practice was three hours a night. It was hard, but we'd gotten to the top team and were both happy to be there.

As the other girls on our team started to arrive, we made our way out to the floor for warm-ups. Greg expected us to warm up on our own and we all knew what to do. He made his way out to the floor to help us stretch after he grabbed something to eat.

"How's it going, T?" he asked as he leaned over and pushed on my hips while I tried like hell to get to the floor on my right split.

I suck at flexibility.

"Ugh, how's it look like it's going?" I asked with a smile.

We split into two groups, and Tracy and I went to the platform to work on double fulls. I almost had mine, but the repetition was key. Round off, back handspring, set, pull, do a double full. I could hear Greg's voice in my head: "You set and you pull, and you do a double full."

Greg came over after I had done about twenty.

"Those are looking good, T. Now tell me you love me and you can get down," he said matter-of-factly.

I stood on the platform in my neon leotard with my permed blond eighties hair, sway-backed posture, and cocky attitude, and looked down at him.

What did he just say? I blinked my eyes and my steps stuttered a bit as I processed the situation.

Greg's blue eyes twinkled with playfulness, while the six-foot-one-inch, two hundred and twenty pounds of protein powder-fueled muscular hulk of him just stood there in front of me, looking up, refusing to move.

As if hearing my internal question, he repeated, "You can't get down until you tell me you love me."

"No," I said matter-of-factly…with just a bit of sass.

Why is he doing this? I mean, he's always playing around, but this is weird.

"T, you're not getting down until you tell me you love me."
The playfulness was replaced with something else. I didn't have
words for it, but it didn't feel good.

I laughed uncomfortably and said no again.

He laughed a little too. "You know you love me, T. Just say
it."

I wanted to get to the next event. *Why is he being like this?*
Why is he paying so much attention to me? I wish he would just get
out of my way!

He stood there, refusing to move until the words came out of
my mouth.

Fine, I thought.

"I love you." I said it—quickly and awkwardly and with a
few ounces of smart-ass, but I said it. And when my stomach
turned, I thought back to when we had traveled to Australia and, in
order to be cool and liked, I had succumbed to his challenge of
eating a raw oyster. A few hours later, I vomited, and that taste of
vomit made a swift appearance in my mouth again as I leapt off the
platform and headed to my next event.

Why does he act like that? And why wouldn't he just leave
me alone when I said NO?

Danielle and Tracy met me at the water fountain to get a
quick drink before the next event.

Tracy saw something in my expression and asked, "What's
wrong?"

"Nothing. Greg's just being weird." I tried to brush off the
discomfort I felt.

"Well, that's normal for him, right?" Tracy said with a
wink. She had been on Greg's team a year longer than I had and
seemed to understand him. She had also gotten a lot closer with
Samantha, another girl on the team who was a year older than me.
The infamous Samantha, with her thin athletic frame, warm brown
eyes, clear Irish skin, and soft brown hair. She was an amazing
gymnast who I couldn't come close to competing with, and I
wasn't sure where I stood with either of them. I was pretty sure
Samantha didn't like me.

"Remind me to tell you something later," Tracy said as we walked back out into the gym together to vault.

Hmm. I wonder what that's about. Seems important.

Vault, bars, beam, floor; that was the routine. Ten years I had spent at this gym practicing and practicing, and I was now a Level 8 Optional. (That year, gymnastics categories changed from a "class" system to a "level" system and what had been Class II became a Level 8.) I'd been on Greg's team for a few months now, along with some of my other friends who had also moved up. We were the highest-level girls team in the gym, and there were nine of us from Level 8 to Level 10. I mostly liked the advanced team, but I felt like I had to work harder than the other girls to learn the same skills. I was strong, but I still struggled with flexibility; and some things just didn't come as easily for me as for the others.

Danielle and Tracy are both talking about quitting. Can I do this without them? I've been putting more and more hours in the gym but it seems like I am still struggling to keep up. And then I wondered what I would do if not for this gym. *Gymnastics is tough, but the reality is that home is even worse.*

When my Mom married Bob, I suddenly had three adult parents all acting like teenagers.

Dad didn't pay Mom back for my doctor's visit, and Mom was stressed about money. Bob hasn't spoken to me, for some reason, for the last several days, and Mom has been cold, and I don't even know why. Dad still wants me to come live with him and Derek, and though he may not say it, I feel his hurt.

There were short periods of peace, but it always seemed like one of the three of them was upset about something. They didn't talk about it much, but they didn't necessarily hide it either.

I hate the way it feels at home.

I was living with a man I barely knew, and my Dad and brother were still twenty minutes away in my old house, and what felt like a different life. Sometimes, I still spent the first twenty minutes at the gym in the shower stall telling Tracy or Danielle the latest drama between my parents and crying a lot there too, though it seemed like Tracy was off with Samantha more often. Tracy had built new friendships since she'd moved up a level the year before me.

I still don't feel like I can trust anyone at school except for Lilly, and now she's gone to high school. Maybe it's because all they want to do is go to the mall, and talk about their new Benetton jeans and IOU sweatshirts? There are some nice girls, but I always feel like an outsider. I don't belong here. I am so mean and bitchy to my Mom, Dad, and Derek, but I can't seem to keep that anger back.

School is tough, but also a way for me to dive in and lose myself in the work, so I get good grades.

I just never feel comfortable—not at home, not at school, and now even the gym? No way. Why is Greg acting like that? It seems like more and more friends are quitting to run track or do cheerleading, something a little easier than gymnastics.

My brain snapped back to the vault as I heard Tracy say, "T, you're up. Are you sure you're okay?"

"Yeah, I'm good. Sorry." I hadn't been paying attention and it was my turn to vault. I ran down and did a warm-up vault of a "half on" to make sure my board was set right and I had my run dialed. I had enough height coming off that I knew I could do a Tsuk next. These one and a half rotations off the vault after doing a handspring half twist from the springboard made me feel powerful when I did them.

"More shoulders, T. Really explode out of your shoulders," Greg coached as he held his arms up and mimicked the motion he wanted me to focus on. He grabbed my shoulders and squeezed as I started to walk away.

"Here, practice on me," he said and put his hands up in the air over my head. I knew the drill and put my hands up to touch his and then leaned forward a little. He pressed weight down on my hands so that I wouldn't fall, and I pushed my shoulders up fast and strong to try to move his hands. "Harder," he said. I pushed again. "Three more," he said. Pop, pop, pop. I felt his weight release and I dropped my arms. "That's better, T, really pop out of those shoulders and you have this."

"Got it." I turned and headed back to the end of the runway. On my way, my mind flashed back to a few weeks before when I had worn a two-piece leotard to the gym. There was no rule against it, but Greg kept asking to touch my abs that day, and talking about how much he liked them. I could feel him leaning over me and rubbing my stomach with his big huge hand, once I finally gave in and let him touch me. *I won't be wearing that two-piece again,* I thought, as I got back in line behind Tracy. *He's so weird.*

Greg always stood next to the vault in case anyone needed a spot. My teammates and I were all at the end of the vault runway, far enough away that he couldn't hear our conversations and we couldn't hear his. Danielle and I were both working on a tsukahara, which meant that we hit the springboard with our feet, did a half twist and a half rotation, hit the vault with our hands, did one and a half somersaults, and then (hopefully) landed on our feet. As I stood in line waiting, again my thoughts wandered.

Do I have to go to Dad's this weekend? All this back and forth on the weekends sucks. I'm not friends with anyone in Salem anymore, and when I go down there all I do is watch a bunch of TV in the house that used to be my home. Whew! It's my turn, enough thinking about it.

"Do you want a spot?" Greg asked.

"Just a light one," I said.

I set my feet on my start line and did my little "step hop" that started off my run. I sprinted to the vault and pop, pop, pop! I felt his hands on my low back and stomach for just a split second in the middle of the air. My 90-pound body made a powerful sound when hitting the board, the vault, and the ground. Greg had barely touched me—I had not needed a spot.

"You got this, T. It's really looking great," he said as he hugged me. I started to pull away from the sweaty hulk of him, but he pulled me in just a little tighter, and then let go.

"Thanks," I smiled and something made me feel like things were okay again.

That's the supportive and loving Greg I know. He seems to really know when I need a hug. He was fifteen years younger than my parents, but fifteen years older than me, and he seemed to have it all figured out. He was goofy and weird, but he was so confident. *If my family doesn't act like they love me, at least he does. I don't know why he made me say that I love him, but I guess I really do. Why would he want me to tell him I loved him if he didn't love me? I know he wouldn't pay this much attention to me and talk to me this much if he didn't like me and think I was smart. He's always telling me how smart I am and how I get concepts so much faster than the other girls. He is always asking about Dad and Derek and encouraging me to keep an eye on them. He even cares about my family. He loves me. I know it.*

I trotted back down to the end of the vault runway as Danielle did her Tsuk. Tracy was waiting for me with questions. "Hey, how's that guy in your English class? Matt, right?"

"Ugh! Dreamy, but he doesn't even know my name," I said with a big sigh.

Boys. I don't know the first thing.

"Why do you think he doesn't know your name?" Tracy smiled and tilted her head as she asked.

"Well that's an exaggeration. He borrows pencils from me and stuff, so he probably does know my name, but he has no idea that I like him," I said, turning a little red just thinking about it.

Matt is the first guy I have ever REALLY liked. He's hot, and smart, and athletic, and totally too cool for me, I thought as Tracy prepped for her vault.

Watching her vault, I couldn't help but notice how Greg didn't hug her like he did me. She stepped off the mat almost as soon as she landed and he just said a few words to her.

Huh, that's not how he treats me.

Next thing I knew she was by my side again and I asked, "What about you? Who's your latest boy?" Boys were a safe and entertaining topic at this age, Tracy's especially. She was one of few gymnasts who wore a bra size bigger than A.

"I'm dating Rick now," she said.

"The Rick that bought you the Milli Vanilli album? I thought you didn't like him." My tone was a little surprised and maybe judgy.

"Eh, he won me over. And, he can drive," Tracy said with a mischievous smile.

I smiled back at her. "Hehe. That is a plus," I said as I thought, *I'd never date someone just because they could drive. She's so confident. Maybe that's what happens when you get to high school.*

"I think you should tell Matt you like him, or just ask him to do something with you," Tracy said with a wide-eyed challenge.

"What? I can't do that. What would I say?" My cheeks flushed and my heart raced at the mere thought of asking Matt to do something with me.

Tracy's only a year older than me. Why is she so much more comfortable with this stuff?

Samantha chimed in, "Yeah, Torey, ask him out."

"Right," I said with a sarcastic smirk, but there was something about the way Samantha said it that made me feel like she was making fun of me.

She's got a year on me too, I thought. *Maybe next year I'll be confident enough to ask Matt out. I'll be in high school then. Maybe then I won't feel so nervous all the time. Maybe then I'll fit in.*

It was my turn to vault again so I had a great excuse to get out of the conversation. I stepped up to the line that I always started from and looked down the runway to Greg standing at the end. He was looking at me with a question, "Spot?"

"Just be there." I was pretty good at this vault already, but there was always that chance that my hand would slip or something, and I didn't want to get hurt. An injury could ruin my whole competitive year.

"You got it, T," he said.

I step-hopped into my run and charged down the runway. I felt Greg's hand graze my chest in the air, but he didn't actually move me at all. I had done it totally by myself and I had stuck it. When I looked up at him, he was smiling. "T, that was all you!"

"But I felt you touch me," I said, a little perturbed. I wanted that Tsuk all for myself and I felt like his touch took that away from me.

"I didn't help you at all," he said as he wrapped his arms around me from behind, and gave me a big hug. "You did it, T! I'm so proud of you."

"Thanks," I said, still a little irked.

It feels good to know I have a skill like this already and I've only been on his team for a few months. Maybe I can get a college scholarship.

Practice was almost over, and we all went out for a water break before starting on our conditioning. Tracy had invited me to her house after practice, and I was excited to go because she and I hadn't spent much time together in a while. It seemed like she was always with Samantha.

Later that afternoon, we were sitting on her bed listening to Run DMC on her silver boom box in her little upstairs bedroom. I could hear some of the many birds that her grandma kept, even over Run DMC.

Those birds are loud, I'll never own a pet bird.

We were sitting on her bed making friendship bracelets, and having fun joking around. I felt just like I used to with her, like I could trust her with anything and that she was a solid friend.

"Torey, I need to tell you something," Tracy said in sort of a whisper.

This sounds serious.

"Okay," I said.

"Samantha and Greg are sleeping together." Her head was down, except for a quick glance at her door.

"What? Really?" My furrowed brow translated that I was surprised if not shocked. I got kind of sweaty and my heart sped up.

I know Samantha is Greg's favorite, that's obvious, but this is crazy news. Why is she telling me this? Samantha would hate it if she knew I knew.

"Yeah, Samantha told me a while ago, but I'm not telling you to be a gossip. I just don't know how long I am going to be around. I think I am going to quit gymnastics before the next season, and I wanted you to know. I don't want you to get sucked in." Tracy looked right into my eyes.

"Ugh, I won't, that's gross!" I exclaimed.

Seriously, gross. I can't even begin to imagine being with Greg. He is OLD. He's more like a dad or an uncle than a guy I would date.

"That's what I think, too, but Samantha says she's in love with him. She told me she'd hate me if I told anyone, but I just want you to know so that you can watch out. I've seen the way he talks to you. I wouldn't want to see you fall into something too."

"Don't worry. I won't say anything to Samantha. Thanks for telling me, Tracy. I'm glad you trust me, and I won't break that trust," I promised as my mind exploded with what this all meant.

Chapter Four:
Confessions at Camp

Summer 1991

The summer between my freshman and sophomore year of high school, a group of us went to a summer gymnastics camp in Hershey, Pennsylvania. Greg drove, and we met the other coach and his team at the gym in the early evening. This was not at a true camp with horses, swimming, crafts and photography, but just another gymnastics center like ours, which meant a lot more work than play. We would be staying at the homes of the other gymnasts, and we had yet to find out our bunk arrangements. There was a clear pecking order on the team, and everyone knew their place. Samantha and Jill were the best gymnasts and, from my perspective at least, the coolest girls on the team. Jill was four years older than me and would be going to Rutgers at the end of the summer. She and I got along well, and I loved her to death, but she was more my idol than my friend. Tracy and Samantha were best friends by then and they hung out all the time, just like Tracy and I used to. I was a little sad about it, but Danielle and I were closer and a few of the other younger girls on the team were close friends too. I was hoping to bunk with Danielle, but I would be happy to be with Jill, Samantha, or Tracy too.

I just don't want to be alone.

I had never really liked sleep-away camps ever since I was violently homesick at 4-H camp when I was eight. It made my stomach turn a bit just to think about being alone with a family and a gymnast I didn't know.

When we pulled into the gravel parking lot of the gym after the four-and-a-half-hour drive, all of us were ready to pop out of that van and into the fresh night air. There were several cars in the lot parked haphazardly and some girls as well as parents were milling around talking. Their attention turned to us as the giggling playful group of us poured out of the van.

As we wiggled around in an obvious "not from here" group just outside the van, waiting to be assigned a place to sleep, Greg started calling out names, "Samantha, Tracy, and Jill, you all go with Cindy."

Cindy raised her hand and met them, and I watched as they excitedly said their "Hellos" and started to load their things into her family's van.

Bummer.

"Danielle and Katie, you go with Debbie," Greg announced.

Double bummer. I'm either with one of the younger girls, or ALONE.

I stood there last picked, feeling like a total loser.

There was some discussion between the coaches and then Tracy's mom jumped out of her van and joined the discussion. Right after that, Greg walked over to me.

"T, you're going to be staying with Marissa, but she and her family are out of town until tomorrow, so you can go to Cindy's tonight too. They have a lot of room," he said, smiling at me in a knowing way.

"Okay."

Sweet, I thought as I grabbed my bag and joined Samantha, Tracy, and Jill in the van to go to Cindy's house.

I was so happy as I climbed in and sat next to Samantha.

I'm with the cool kids, I thought. *This is awesome.*

Cindy was sixteen, and a Level 10 like Samantha and Jill. They shared some thoughts on what skills they'd be working on this week, but the talk quickly turned from gymnastics to music and movies and normal teenage banter. Cindy seemed like she'd be fun to know.

Maybe this will be more fun than I thought.

I had just turned fourteen and it was fun to be with all the older girls.

When we got there, it was getting late and they immediately showed us the sleeping options. There was a set of bunk beds in one room that Tracy and Jill immediately called dibs on (they didn't have bunk beds at home and were apparently very excited about them).

"Cindy is sleeping in her own room because I want her to do her best this week and not be up all-night yakking with you all," Cindy's mom said with a smile. "Samantha, you and Torey can have the screened-in patio."

I walked out behind Samantha and saw the two twin beds and the lovely big green trees just beyond.

I love it! It's like we are practically outside.

We took our bags out to our beds, got our pajamas on, and then went back in to quickly brush our teeth. Samantha and I said goodnight to the other girls and headed out to the night air of the patio.

I thought that Samantha and I were "friends" on the surface, but it didn't always feel like it inside. I felt like I was only cool enough to hang out with her if there wasn't someone else around. Lying there in the quickly cooling night, I was sure she was bummed that she wasn't in the other room with Tracy or Jill. For several minutes, I laid there quietly listening to crickets with the sticky summer breeze blowing over me. I knew that practice started at eight the next morning, and we were looking at six to eight hours in the gym each day.

It's going to be a tough week. Can I keep up? Will I be able to hack it? My mind always seemed to doubt my abilities.

I was surprised when Samantha asked quietly, "Are you awake?"

"Yeah. I'm nervous, and can't really sleep," I said honestly.

"Why are you nervous, T?" she asked, just like someone who has never been nervous and never doubted her abilities.

"I don't know, I just feel like everyone's better than me and I'm not going to be able to keep up." It was painful to admit it, but it was the truth.

Not good enough, never good enough.

"Everyone's not better than you. You're doing great. You've only been at this level for a year. Give it some time, Torey."

"Thanks, Samantha. I'm trying."

"There's something I've been wanting to tell you," she said with just the slightest hint of hesitation.

"Tell me," I prodded, interested and surprised that she wanted to talk to me.

Oh, boy, what's this about? Did I do something to make her mad?

"Greg and I are together." She said it quietly but matter-of-factly.

Holy shit, really?! She's telling me this? I'm not supposed to know.

"What do you mean, together?" I asked, playing dumb and hoping she couldn't tell I wasn't being honest.

Why is she telling me this? My heart was racing and I rolled over to face her and look at her eyes.

"We love each other. He told me that he'd wait until I am eighteen and marry me. We've been together for a while." She sounded proud as she said it and as if just saying it out loud made it mean more. This was no high school fling.

"What? Really?" I asked with enough surprise because I was literally floored by the marriage thing.

Really? He would wait for her? I wonder what 'a while' means? At least a year, because that's when Tracy told me. I wonder if she knows how he talks to me?

"Yeah." She rolled over and up on her elbow to face me.

"Like you are WITH him?" I asked, trying to act the way I would have if I didn't already know.

I need clarification. I probably sound like a naïve idiot.

"Yeah, WITH him." She emphasized the WITH just like I

had and then laughed a little uncomfortably.

My heart was still racing. Even though Tracy had told me, and I knew, the words coming out of her mouth created a feeling in the pit in my stomach that told me it was not okay.

Hearing it from her makes it not just real, but now I am a part of the secret. Play dumb, play dumb. What other questions should I ask?

"Did you consider marrying him?" I am sure I sounded like a little girl.

"No." There was a palpable pause and her voice wavered a little. "I told him not to wait for me." She swallowed hard. I could tell she was having a hard time talking about this, but she kept going. "That's why he's dating Marylou, but he still loves me and we are still together. After I told him that I wouldn't marry him, things got more serious with Marylou, but nothing ever stopped with us."

I took a deep breath and collected my nerves.

Why am I anxious about this? Sure, Greg has told me some sexual stories, but this has nothing to do with me.

"So, you're doing it?" I asked as innocently as I could, but felt like the naïve, not-quite-high school, girl that I was.

"Well, yeah," she shot back with a little edge and a condescending laugh.

Holy shit, I can't believe she told me.

"Like, all the way?" I asked.

I'm naïve, I know, but I need to know the truth.

"Yeah. All the way, Torey. Geez." In the little bit of light we had, I could see her roll her eyes.

"Okay. Okay. I just want to be sure I totally understand. Does anyone else know?"

I must be cool or she wouldn't trust me with this.

"Tracy knows, but that's it."

"Okay," I paused really wondering what led to this disclosure. "So why are you telling me?"

"I don't know. I like you, and I just thought you should know. Greg really likes you and he trusts you too, so I thought I should tell you. It's obviously not something that people can know. Nobody would understand. I know you do though." As she said it, I felt as if she was not only asking me to keep her secret, but letting me know she was watching Greg and me. I wanted to believe I was just cool, and this wasn't a way for her to stay a little safer in her situation.

I must be totally "in" with Samantha now or she wouldn't have told me. She trusts me. We really ARE friends. I know Greg cares about me too. In fact, maybe I'm even more special because we have a platonic relationship. He must respect me and love me more since he doesn't hook up with me.

"When you love someone, you love them, right?" I asked trying to sound supportive, or at least like I hadn't known for a year already and felt kind of worried about it all.

"Yeah, and I really love him. I love how good he is. I love that he doesn't drink or smoke or swear. I love how big he is and how he can so easily pick me up. I love how he holds me and how he kisses me. I love how he smells and the way he is always so funny and crazy. I love that he makes me laugh. I love how safe I feel when I am with him. I KNOW he loves me. I've never felt love like this. And he's totally hot, isn't he? I mean, I LOVE his body."

Well, I disagree. I wouldn't call Greg "hot." I mean, he's a body builder, so there's that, and we gymnasts appreciate muscles, but he's OLD. He's 15 years older than me. Weird. He is NOT HOT.

"He does have awesome muscles," I said as honestly as I could. "So, Marylou doesn't know anything?" I asked, wondering how they could have possibly kept this a secret for so long.

"No, Greg told me she wouldn't understand. He says that I am his first choice, but he wants to get married and have a family, so if I'm not willing to marry him, he has to find a wife. He says we'll have to stop being together if they get married, but he loves me and he knows I love him, so it's okay. What we do is what people who love each other do. We just have to keep it quiet." She sounded tired. Like just telling me this story was hard on her and kind of a big deal.

"Yeah, I guess that makes sense. Well, you can trust me, Samantha. I won't tell anyone, I promise," I said sincerely.

She'd hate me forever if I told anyone. I am "in" now and I don't have to act like I don't know. I am one of TWO of her friends who know. She hasn't even told Jill. This is a game changer.

The next morning, I woke up before her. I put on my leotard and shorts and went to the bathroom. When I came back into the patio room, she was awake and dressed. She stood up and gave me a big hug.

This is NOT normal Samantha.

"Thanks for listening last night," she said.

"Of course, you can trust me," I promised as I hugged her back. "We're leaving in fifteen minutes, so let's go grab some breakfast."

"Okay, I'll be right behind you," she said as she sat back down on the bed.

I packed up my things since I had to move to a different house that night, and grabbed a bagel with butter and strawberry jam from the kitchen. After I said good morning to Cindy, Jill, and Tracy, I threw a banana in my gym bag and headed to the van.

That day in the gym, it was as if everything had changed. I was on the same social level as Tracy, Samantha, and Jill. I was in their group. I was included in the conversations. I was encouraged on the skills I was working on. I was "in." But I couldn't get all this out of my head.

SHE is his GIRLFRIEND? How can he treat us all fairly if he is WITH her? How is this really happening and no one knows? I thought it was true when Tracy told me, but now it seems so much more real and so much more wrong. I'm not sure why Samantha telling me makes it so different in my head. What do I do with this? It's so obvious now. It reminds me of when Mom told me about my parents' divorce; from that day on, there was constant fighting at our house. It's like I can suddenly see EVERY interaction differently. Every time he hugs her, or spots her, when she might not really need it. It's so glaringly obvious now.

Chapter Five:
Hallucinating on the High Bar

Winter 1991

I was on the high bar about to cast to a handstand when he looked up at me, said "55," and winked. I smiled at him, knowing that's what he expected when he used our "inside jokes," but there was a pit in my stomach at the same time. I knew exactly what he was talking about, but no one else around me did. It seemed like Samantha didn't even know what "55" meant or he wouldn't have said it when she was right there. So much had happened since camp, including Greg getting engaged to Marylou.

I casted to a handstand, and then fell over the other side of the bar.

Damn those giants! If he's not holding my wrist, I can never do them. I hate mental blocks! Why do I NEED Greg?

As I walked to the chalk bucket and re-chalked my grips, I remembered back to the day he told me the "55" story.

It was a summer day and Greg approached me when I first got to the gym. "I have a new technique I want to try on your low back."

I almost always had pain in my low back, supposedly because my abs were weak and my posture was bad. Greg had been studying chiropractic and he would try the different adjustments that he learned on me. No one ever questioned it. Why would they?

"Okay." I followed him around the platform to the back of the gym.

It was a hot day and Greg had already been at the gym for a few hours teaching classes. He took me to the stack of blue Velcro blocks in the back of the gym behind the platform. I knew the drill, and "assumed the position" of lying on my side, with my upper leg bent and my body just slightly twisted. Greg then leaned over me with his left hand on my left shoulder and his right hand on my left upper hip.

We had done this a hundred times, but today was different. He was taking more time than usual to set me up, apparently, because this was a new technique that he hadn't used before. We were the only ones in the back of the gym.

"How's Matt doing?" he asked with a twinkle in his eye that told me he wanted details.

"Great! He's the best. I totally LOVE him," I gushed.

"Do you kiss him with tongue?" His tone was challenging.

I turned a little red. "Yeah…"

Why does he ask me stuff like that?

"Have you put your mouth on him yet?" He leaned over and whispered the question in my ear. .

"No! Ew," I shot back and made a gagging face.

Seriously? Greg loves to make me feel uncomfortable. Why does it seem like he is always pushing me a little further on this topic? It used to just be about me and my body? Now that I am dating Matt, it's more and more about sex.

"Ok, breathe in," he said, and I took a big deep breath. "And out." He pressed the weight of his body on to mine and I heard the usual snap, crackle, pop, that always made him happy.

"You know that's what people who love each other do, right?" he asked.

"Not yet in my world, and that may never happen," I blushed, and he laughed at me again. I rolled over to the other side.

"I had a girlfriend that would do it while I was driving 55 miles per hour," he said quietly but proudly. "It was amazing," he whispered softly in my ear.

As he said this, I could feel the weight of him on top of me again, and smell the combination of his sweat and the chalk in the air of the gym. I heard my back crack and his satisfied, "Ha! I got it. I always struggle with that side, but I got them both today!"

He was like a happy little kid, but my heart was racing and I wanted to crawl out of my skin. I wanted to run away but I laid there frozen.

Why does he tell me this shit?

"Roll over on your back and just stay there for a few minutes, T. Let's see if we can keep that low back in place for a while. Get started warming up when you're ready," he said as turned and walked away.

I rolled onto my back and stared up at the ceiling of the gym. The white material had hundreds of holes and cracks in it from when the gym used to be tennis courts and the balls would hit it. I looked for pictures in the cracks.

Mr. Magoo, a bunny, North America, a star, penis. Ew, why am I thinking about penises now? He must really trust me to tell me these things about his life, right? For God's sake, he's engaged to be married. He must care about me to confide in me this way. Right? That's why he tells me this stuff, to teach me how to be with my boyfriend and what adults do when they are sexual? I wonder if he talks to Samantha about this stuff. I wonder if he teaches her how to do it?

After about ten minutes of lying there wondering why Greg told me stuff like this, and trying to ignore the visual of a woman giving him a blow job while he was driving down the freeway, I reluctantly got up and went out on the floor and started my warm up.

My mind came back to the present and working on my stupid giants when Tracy nudged me that it was my turn. I skipped up on the low bar, casted, put my feet on the low bar, and jumped to the high bar.

"Can I have a spot?" I asked.

"Sure, but you know you have it," Greg said as he climbed up on the same blue blocks on which he adjusted me during the "55" conversation. I was perched on the high bar waiting and he put his right hand around my left wrist. I casted to a handstand, feeling strong and secure. I knew he had me if I peeled. I swung down, kicked my feet back below the low bar, and then kicked hard in front so that my body inverted again up into a handstand and on top of the bar.

Giants feel so cool. Why can't I just do them without him? Why do I have to freak out and let go? Why do I always see myself peeling if he's not touching my stupid wrist?

That's typically all it took. As long as Greg's hand was on my wrist, I could do giant after giant after giant. As soon as that hand was gone, I either fell over the top, or dropped off half-way through. I couldn't visualize myself doing an entire giant by myself. I saw myself peel off and break my neck every time. It was a mental block and no one could help me with it. I just couldn't do it without him.

What is wrong with me? I have every physical ability to do this, why can't I just do it? I am just NOT GOOD ENOUGH!

Chapter Six:
Reeling at the Rest Stop

Spring 1992

I sat against the wall on the folded bleachers in front of the beam, visualizing my routine again and again. My small green bag sat next to me with my grips, tape, warm ups, and notebook for scorekeeping in it. This was it. My last event. I had 26.7 after floor, vault, and bars, averaging and 8.9 out of 10 on each event, *pretty damn good*. All my routines had been solid so far, and beam was my best event.

I've got this. There's no way I won't get the 34.0 all-around I need to qualify to nationals. I've got this.

Glancing up at the line of teammates, I saw one of the moms braiding her daughter's hair and suddenly felt sad. My mind flashed back to church the week before…

"Parents, please come stand behind your child who is being confirmed," Betty Sue, our pastor, said.

I was kneeling next to Lilly on the red carpeted steps of the First Presbyterian Church, experiencing our official confirmation ceremony. I heard the shuffling of parents getting out of their seats and then, to my surprise and embarrassment, I saw my Dad storm out of the door at the front of the sanctuary as Mom and Bob stood behind me. I bowed my head, and the humiliation of my father walking out caused acid to rise in my throat and tears to tumble down my cheeks.

Why can't they think about me for once? Why do they have to act like children? It's church, for God's sake! Everyone just saw that. I hate it when they act like this!

"Torey, you're up next! Are you ready?" One of my teammates nudged my arm and brought me back to prepping for the beam routine that would qualify me for the biggest gymnastics meet of my life.

Nationals. I've got this. Church was a week ago. My parents are idiots. Whatever. It doesn't matter.

I sat up straighter and visualized my routine in my mind one last time: cartwheel on, back handspring, back handspring one arm, switch leg leap, front flip with one and a half twists to dismount. I had done this routine hundreds of times without falling, at least forty times a week for the last six months.

There's no way I can possibly screw this up.

I looked up just in time to see Samantha dismounting. She stuck it. I smiled and clapped for her. "Good job, Samantha!" I yelled with a smile.

I was up.

I adjusted the springboard and checked the mats one last time before wiping some chalk between my hands, and then just a little on the ball of each foot. I could feel the adrenaline rising inside me, and the sweat start to darken the armpits of my leotard. I stood at the far end of the beam shaking my hands and bouncing up and down, eagerly awaiting the judges' signal.

"Go, T!" my teammates cheered. Brianna, Samantha, Christina, and Sam were all sitting on the bleachers to my left. "Let's go, Torey!" they called out enthusiastically.

Greg grabbed the top of my shoulders and squeezed. "You

got this, T. No problem."

I smiled up at him, but my heart was racing.

I'm ready to be done with this event.

As much as I loved beam, it was always so nerve-wracking compared to the other quicker and more powerful events, and I HATED when it was our last event. Still, I couldn't be more physically prepared for this.

I've got this, I've got this, I've got this.

Finally, the judges were done with Samantha's score. Her 9.3 easily qualified her for nationals (again), and probably earned her a first-place medal. I clapped for her, and whistled with the rest of my teammates.

I looked down at my feet to focus, and when I looked up, the head judge raised her arm.

Here goes!

I offered my BIG smile, raised my right hand at her, stepped to the left, saluted the other judge, and then stood still just for a second like a little toy soldier before starting my sprint to the board. Boom, cartwheel on.

Crap! Too much power.

I knew it just before I hit the beam.

Seriously, I fell off on my SUPER EASY mount!? What the hell? What's wrong with me? That's 0.5 off my score. My mind was racing. *Okay, Torey, get your shit together and DO THIS! If you're quitting this year anyway, let's at least end this career with a trip to Nationals. Shit.*

I took the split-second I had to breathe and pull myself together, then I jumped back up on the beam, heart racing, hands shaking, not even hearing my teammates cheering from the sidelines.

One thing at a time. I coached myself. *Turn, jump, stretch, spin. Set up for my flight move.*

I put the ball of my right foot into the arch of my left and the palm of my right hand into the groove between my left index finger and thumb, took a deep breath, and swung my arms down and then back up. Back handspring, back handspring one arm.

Shit! In another split-second, I was on the floor. *I can't control the energy. This is BAD. If I fall again, I might not get the 7.3 I need to make it to Nationals.*

That acidic feel in my throat from church last week returned and the tears started.

I can't just sit here and cry. I shook my head. *I have to get back up there and finish. God, I suck. I can't believe I fell twice already.*

I took a deep breath and jumped back up onto the beam, tears running down my cheeks.

Get. It. Together. Torey.

I didn't have much left in my routine, but that didn't matter because in that state, I could barely walk on the beam, let alone do an easy turn or jump. Four feet high, four inches wide, sixteen feet long – the beam that used to be my place of stability and strength was kicking my ass all over the place.

I set up for my one and a half turn and my toe caught as I spotted the end. I was off again.

That's it. I won't make nationals now.

I climbed back up on the beam and went through the motions to finish my routine, but I was crushed. I was sobbing as I landed my dismount, barely saluted the judges, and ran out of the gym. As I sat there in the cool dark hallway berating myself, it felt good to be alone and no longer up on display for all of the world to witness my failure.

This is how my competitive gymnastics career ends. I totally SUCK.

A blurry and tearful hour later, Samantha found me in the bathroom and gave me a big hug. "It's time to go. Greg is taking you and Brianna and me. It's going to be okay."

I accepted her hug, but I felt like a pile of mush as I walked back into the gymnasium.

I missed awards. I didn't even cheer for my teammates. I suck.

I packed up my grips, notebook, and warm ups, and threw on my favorite Hatteras t-shirt and jeans over my leotard before quietly following Samantha out to the car in the rain.

I couldn't even look at my friends as I hopped in the car…and especially not at him.

It was a cold spring day in Ohio and the heater in the car didn't work, so we had blankets. Brianna was in the back seat, and Samantha and Greg flanked me on the bench seat. Samantha had her arm around me, and Greg was holding my hand under the blanket. I just sat there, practically comatose, not even blinking with the stutter of the broken windshield wiper.

I can't believe that just happened.

The pit in my stomach grew. I was so sick about my failure, I couldn't even speak, nor did I want to. In this car, everyone already knew, and they understood how much it mattered to me. I didn't need to talk now. It was muggy in the car and my hand that Greg held was sweaty, no longer from anxiety about the beam, but now from anxiety about telling everyone that I didn't make it to Nationals. The weather paralleled my overwhelming need to pour out tears and heartache; but I was so exhausted, I had to just breathe for a while.

"That windshield wiper is going to scratch the glass," Greg said as he pulled to the side of the road. He took his shoe and sock off, but I was too distracted by my immense failure to even wonder why. After putting his shoe back on without the sock, he got out of the car in the pouring rain, and ran around to the passenger side's broken wiper, tied his sock around it, and then ran back around to his seat.

I felt his wet, cold skin as he reached back under the blanket to grab my hand and squeeze.

This is bizarre, I thought. *Samantha doesn't even seem jealous that he's holding my hand. I must be that pathetic—they just feel bad for me.*

We stopped at a rest stop to use the bathroom, and I needed to call my Dad. I felt sick as I ran through the rain and inside to the phone booth.

I am such a failure.

Crying again, I leaned against the side of the booth to try to collect myself.

I have to get it together to call Dad.

My head was bowed in defeat when I saw his wet high-top Nikes with the bandana tied around one walk right up to my Adidas.

Giving me no time to react, Greg tipped my chin up, and kissed me on the mouth.

Holy shit! He just did that.

It was fast, but different than a puckered kiss that a mom or dad would give. It was soft, and illicit even though it was fast. It was not to be seen or acknowledged by anyone but me. My heart was racing again and I didn't know what to feel. Surprise, anger, hurt, flattery, love, satisfaction, and confusion swirled in my mind. I knew it was not innocent, and the length of the hug that he gave me immediately after confirmed it. This was not fatherly. He had finally crossed the physical line.

WHAT THE…? THAT just happened. HE DID IT. HE kissed ME. Holy shit! I never ever thought that would happen. Jesus. Okay, shit, now what? I could feel his huge arms around me. I was sobbing and he was just holding me. *He's so strong. I am such a failure, but at least Greg still loves me. I can't believe he just kissed me on the mouth.*

"I'll see you back at the car. I love you, T. It's all going to be okay," he reassured me as he kissed my head and walked into the men's room.

Seriously? It's all going to be okay? Greg, who are you kidding? I just failed in my last attempt to make a national meet I should have qualified for time and again. Not only are you married with a kid, but you are sleeping with Samantha, AND YOU JUST KISSED ME ON THE MOUTH. What about ANY of this is okay? I am so not okay.

Chapter Seven:
Losing Limits at the Lake

Summer 1992

I was standing outside in the driveway of Samantha's dad's house. There was a huge graduation party going on for Samantha's older sister and you could feel the energy and excitement of teenagers with the taste of freedom. It was always fun to hang out with my teammates outside the gym, in a normal social setting. We always joked that we weren't used to seeing each other with our "clothes" on.

I had some lemonade in my hand, but was feeling awkward now because all my teammates had just left. My boyfriend, Matt, was on a trip to Myrtle Beach with his family, so he wasn't with me either. I scanned my surroundings looking for Samantha or some of her friends whose names I at least knew. There were probably fifty or more high school kids in the driveway and out in the backyard, the music was louder all of a sudden, and the energy level cranked up a notch with the music. You could almost touch the excitement of this graduating class so ready to get out of rural Ohio and on to bigger and better things.

Should I still be here? I don't fit in now.

Samantha's dad's house was out in the country and you could only see one or two houses in the distance. There were people all over as my gaze searched for Samantha in the crowds but also in the periphery. There was a huge yard in both the front and back of the house and there was a tent set up with food and drinks under it, just in case it rained. I didn't see Samantha anywhere.

My mom isn't coming to get me for at least another two hours. Should I go in the house and call her? Ugh, I hate this feeling of not knowing anyone and not fitting in.

Just then, I noticed Greg walking down the road from his car. It was rare to see him out of his "gym clothes."

He looks like such a regular guy in his Z Cavaricci Jeans with his bandana tied around his leg.

He went over and gave the graduate a hug and then walked straight up to me and gave me a similar hug. My heart started to race.

I don't know how to be around him since the kiss. What is this?

"Hey T! Want to go for a walk?" He leaned into me just a little, and smiled down when I looked up at him.

I glanced around for Samantha again.

I don't want her to be mad or jealous.

She must have been preoccupied somewhere with her high school boyfriend, Michael. Without anyone else to hang out with, I didn't even need to make excuses for why I would walk away with Greg.

"Sure," I said, trying not to let my voice waver too much.

We headed out the driveway and my mind flashed back to the aerobics room a few weeks ago.

I was the last one finishing up my conditioning and Greg was with me when I finished my last few minutes on the stationary bike.

When he picked me up and gave me a hug, he whispered, "I love you, T."

"I love you, too." I said the words so much more easily than that time on the platform several years ago, and I was sure I meant them.

"I meant to kiss you, you know," he continued.

I smiled awkwardly and blushed, unable to look at him. We hadn't spoken of it.

He hugged me tight again and kissed my neck. I was startled, and pulled back from the hug, and then he kissed me FOR REAL. With tongue, like Matt did.

I was shocked. Someone could have walked in there any second. But, I couldn't help but kiss him back. His lips were warm and wet and mushier than Matt's, and I got lost in them.

I was startled back to the present moment by his voice, "How's the party been so far?"

We looked both ways and crossed the street while I shook that memory out of my head.

"Pretty good. You just missed Danielle, Tracy, and Brianna. It was good to see Tracy and Danielle. I miss them," I confessed, and relaxed into a nighttime walk with him around the lake. "You ready to go to Iowa?" I asked. He was moving in just a few more weeks, and this time alone with him was precious.

"No, because that means I have to leave you." He reached down and grabbed my hand and squeezed it.

"Whatever," I shot back.

He's so unreal. He can't really mean that. I am NOT that important to him.

"T, you are the Queen, and you know it! My heart is going to hurt every day that I'm away from you. I don't like to think about how much I'm going to miss you." He squeezed my hand again and bumped against me playfully.

"Greg, you have a wife and a son, you have Samantha, you'll be fine," I said with a bit too much power. But in truth I wanted to hear more. I wanted to know that I was important to him too, that I was special. I wanted to be the most special one.

"They aren't the same. YOU are the one I talk to." He pulled me into a side hug. We were in the shadows now, the streetlights not reaching us.

Walking around the far side of the lake, it was getting dark enough to see the stars and the early summer breeze was a little chilly. I was wearing Matt's cutoff button fly Levi's, and a baggy neon Bum Equipment shirt, and I was getting cold. Greg must have noticed me shiver, and took off his jacket and put it on me. It was huge on me, and it smelled like him. I wrapped it tighter around me and then reached back for his hand.

He stopped near a picnic table and I dropped his hand and faced the lake. I was listening to the frogs and looking at the stars.

I love the sound of frogs. Frogs always remind me of Matt. I can't believe I am cheating on him with Greg. I am awful.

Images of Matt, my boyfriend of twelve months, were floating through my mind when Greg came up close behind me and put his arms around me. I leaned back into him. He turned me around and kissed me softly with those big squishy, warm, wet lips.

I should feel so honored that he loves me like this, but I feel guilty. I'm cheating on Matt. He's cheating on his wife AND Samantha. Samantha is my friend. What IS this? What does he mean when he says he loves me? Is this the same kind of love I have for Matt? I don't understand how he can feel that way about Samantha and Marylou and me?

I pulled away from the kiss and snuggled my head into his shoulder.

This feels safer. This feels better.

I just wanted to be with him, as my coach, my friend, my mentor. I didn't want the guilt. He pulled my chin up and kissed me again and I pulled away and turned my back to him.

"What's wrong, T?" he asked, his voice full of concern.

"I don't know." I leaned back against him feeling nervous, but also safe and warm. Looking out into the dark night, I enjoyed the breeze now that I had his coat. I loved being in places like this quiet open space.

In just days, everything is going to change. After Greg leaves, I head to Spain for the World's Fair with the team, and then gymnastics is over for me. My body is done being a gymnast. It's time to transition to diving and see if I can do that through college. I don't want a new gymnastics coach, and my body can't take six more years of this sport anyway.

What is he doing?

I noticed his hands were working their way to my skin. He was touching my abs again. And kissing my neck. My heart was racing. My hormones were raging. I didn't have much sexual experience. Matt was my first boyfriend, and the only guy I'd been with, but my body knew enough to respond to Greg's advances. As his hand moved towards my waistline, I caught my breath.

Where is this going? Is he this bold? He knows that I am totally inexperienced, and he's leaving in a week. What is he doing? These jeans are Matt's and they're loose on my waist. He is NOT ALLOWED to go there.

I moved his hand and turned around.

"Am I making you uncomfortable?" he asked, dumbly.

"Always!" I shot back, blushing, but glad I could stop him that easily.

"You know you like it," he smirked.

Ugh. Greg! Why can't we just keep it good and clean, not wrong and dirty? I love him, but this feels all wrong. I want to be special to him, but I want to keep him as my good coach who supported me and loved me without having to kiss me.

He kissed me again and then pulled me with him as he sat back on the picnic table. He pulled me onto his lap and I faced him. Leaning in and losing myself in the hulk of his chest, I started thinking about all the changes coming for both of us, and started to tear up.

God, I'm going to miss him so much. He's been such a support system for me. Who am I going to lean on now? Who am I going to confide in? What am I going to do without him? Matt is great, but he's just a kid my age trying to figure it out. Greg is older and wiser. And what about no more gymnastics, what does that even look like?

"What's wrong?" he coaxed.

"What am I going to do without you, and the gym?" I pathetically whimpered, and took a deep breath. "Gymnastics is the only constant in my whole life. It's so hard now, but it used to be my only happy place. I'm going to miss it. And, I can't believe you are leaving."

"T, you are so strong. You are going to do awesome at diving. You work so much harder than the other girls, and it's going to pay off. Plus, you have Matt, and I know he loves you…not like I do, but he loves you." He tickled me and made me smile. "You have your Dad and your brother and, I know it's hard, but they need you and you need them. Your mom loves you. Everything is going to be fine. Anyway, who are YOU to talk about change? I'm leaving my whole family except Marylou and Daniel. I'm leaving ALL OF YOU. Plus, I start chiropractic college which is going to be REALLY HARD. If I can do this, then so can you."

He pulled me to him and kissed me again, with tongue, until I pulled back.

"It's all going to be okay," he whispered.

"We'll see." I said softly. "I wonder what time it is? My mom is coming at 10:30."

"I got here around 8:30, so we probably have some time."

"Where's Marylou?" I asked, my guilty conscience getting the better of me.

"She had to stay home to get the baby to bed. I told her I'd be home by 11, so I'll just leave when you do."

"Won't Samantha wonder where you've been all night?" I asked.

"Nah, she's with her friends and Michael. Samantha worries more about Samantha than me," he hugged me and smiled. "That's something I really love about you, T. You worry about me. You think about me. You ask about me. I know you REALLY LOVE me."

"I try." I stuck out my tongue at him.

Sarcasm is much more comfortable.

"Want to head back over to the party and dance?" he asked.

"RIGHT! You know I don't dance." I rolled my eyes at him.

"Well then, let's just stay here and be together for a little longer. I'll try not to make you too uncomfortable, but I just can't help it. I can't keep my hands off your awesome body. I love you so much, I just can't control myself."

I was totally conflicted, but I leaned into it.

I've already cheated on Matt. He's already cheated on Marylou and Samantha. We only have a few weeks left and I want to be special to him. I want him to remember me. I want him to love me. I'm not comfortable with this, but I've already kissed him. What's the harm in doing it more. He's not going below my belt though—that feels too wrong. Maybe he's right, maybe this is what people who love each other do and there's nothing wrong with it. I do love him. But, God, I love Matt so much. I don't know what I'd do without Matt and I so don't want to hurt him. How did this happen? How did I get here? I'm going straight to hell.

Chapter Eight:
Unhindered on the Hideaway Bed

Summer 1992

"My eyes adored you, though I never laid a hand on you, my eyes adored you..." Greg belted out the lyrics right along with Franki Valli and I felt the strength of his arm around me.

Just an hour or so before, Samantha and I were playing Super Mario Brothers and eating popcorn right in front of this same couch. We were at Greg and Marylou's house, which was small; and we sat on the floor in front of the couch, with only a foot or two from our feet to the television. To the right of the television was a stereo system with cassette tapes lying around it. U2, INXS, Talking Heads, a lot of the same music I owned. It was mostly neat in there, save some baby toys laying in the corners, and it was modest (two gymnastics coaches probably don't rake in the dough).

It was hot out, and Samantha and I were in our typical summer attire of shorts and T-shirts. We didn't have practice on Fridays, and earlier that afternoon, my mom dropped me off at Samantha's mom's condo. I told Mom I was spending the night there with Samantha. Samantha's mom wasn't home at the time, and Samantha had told her that she was sleeping over at my house. Of course, Marylou was out of town, and Greg came and picked us both up from Samantha's mom's house around six. He had orchestrated the sleepover, without blatantly asking us to lie—just asking us if we could do it. We didn't have a hard time figuring out a way. It was as if we were perfectly normal teenagers, deceiving our parents, eating popcorn, laughing, and playing stupid video games.

How did we get from there to…here? I wondered as I tried to keep my heart from pounding out of my chest.

Greg was on my left with his arm around me. The lights were low. The hideaway bed was folded out. Samantha was on the other side of him.

We had been sitting there for a while, huddled together, talking about the fact that he was leaving in a few days and the next day was our last practice with him. Samantha and I were sad, but Greg said he was sad, nervous, and excited all at the same time. I, personally, was afraid.

How am I going to do life without Greg and gymnastics?

The conversation ended abruptly when Frankie Valli's song, "My Eyes Adored You," came on. Greg knew every word of the song and sang the whole chorus while Samantha and I leaned our heads against his chest. I listened to the words. I had heard the song before, but this time I REALLY heard the words.

It's ironic, right? He HAD laid a hand on me now.

And, he had laid a lot more than a hand on Samantha. It was as if the emotion and the passion that Franki Valli felt when he wrote the song was surrounding us in the room like a force field.

Is THIS what Franki Valli is singing about? Is this what love is? Is this a special kind of love that people write passionate songs about? Is that what makes it okay for him to be with Samantha?

As the chorus ended, Greg leaned over and kissed Samantha.

Holy shit. I guess he is not worried about me knowing anymore. UGH! This is totally awkward, I mean, I knew they were together, but he's never kissed her in front of me! I squirmed a little not knowing what was going to happen next.

He couldn't possibly think he was going to kiss me in front of Samantha. I mean, she'd be pissed, right?

He could sense my discomfort and pulled me closer to him. "My eyes adored you..." he sang again, as he leaned over and kissed me while Samantha looked on.

Oh my God, this is crazy! What is he doing?!?!

I couldn't believe this was happening. I had not thought this was how this night would go. I thought it might be really fun to be with him and Samantha together. I thought we could all act like there wasn't anything to hide or regret between any of us.

This is NOT what I was expecting.

My heart was racing, and I could feel myself start to sweat. I took a deep breath.

I'm here. I am in this. There's no possibility of jumping up and leaving.

I leaned into it.

What else can I do? He's leaving in a week, and none of this will be an option anymore.

He had moved back to kissing Samantha, but his hand that was at my waist and outside my clothes, moved cautiously onto my skin.

The next thing I knew, his lips were on mine again, and his tongue darted into my mouth this time, while my mind screamed.

What the hell is going on? He's kissing me IN FRONT OF HER!

"All my life, I will remember..." he kept singing, and I kept trying to find my equilibrium.

This is just crazy. What else can I do? I've already kissed him before tonight. Samantha obviously knows and apparently is okay with this. I'm here. I'm in this. This is happening.

He leaned away from me and kissed Samantha again, all the while his hand was working its way under my bra and to my right breast. With my head on his shoulder, I could feel them kissing, but I closed my eyes so I wouldn't see it. It was too intimate to watch. Heart racing, and with a huge lump in my throat, I felt like I might cry. I was sad that he was leaving and completely blown away by what was happening.

Everything is so tainted now. This is so beyond belief. I am going to miss him so much. I don't know what I would have done without him these last few years. I've leaned on him so much. What am I going to do without him? I hate that our relationship has become physical, and I hate that I'm here, but I can't imagine NOT being here either. I mean, he wants me here, right? Samantha wants me here too, or she would have told him not to invite me. There's no longer any tension or competition between us; it's as if this is all okay and normal and we are closer than ever, but I still know it's not okay because I'm so nervous and my stomach hurts. I feel dirty.

He pulled away from her and turned back to kiss me, his right hand all over my upper body. I didn't know what his left hand was doing.

This going away party feels more like a funeral. It's like one big long messed-up, painful goodbye.

The kissing became more and more intense, and longer, with each of us. His hands were constantly moving to give whichever of us he wasn't kissing some attention.

When his hand slipped down between my legs, my stomach turned, so I pulled his hand back up and put it on my stomach. He didn't seem upset by my rejection, and somehow quickly managed to take my bra off with one hand and proceed to touch every inch of skin on my chest. The music was loud enough that none of us felt the need to talk.

*Oh...no...*I thought as I saw Samantha's hand reach for him.

God, I wish it were even darker. I've only ever seen one penis, and I don't want to see Greg's.

The next thing I knew, Samantha slowly grabbed my hand from Greg's chest and tried to move it down.

NO WAY. I pulled my hand away and she sort of laughed.

I felt like the little kid again, but I was not going to let things go that far.

Whatever, Samantha, you might be comfortable going there, but I am not, and I will not. That will forever remain YOUR territory.

Another song came on that he seemed to know by heart, and

he was singing again.

"She's just sixteen years old
Leave her alone, they say
Separated by fools
Who don't know what love is yet
But I want you to know
"If I could fly
I'd pick you up
I'd take you into the night..."
He sang every single word.

Greg does not know the meaning of the word shy. I can't imagine singing in front of anyone. At least when he's singing he's not kissing one of us and I have some time to think.

"I love you two so much," he whispered when the song ended. "I don't know what I am going to do without you. You will write to me, right? And come visit?" He didn't wait for us to respond. "I don't know what I'll do when I don't get to see you both for months!"

He leaned over and kissed Samantha again.

She seemed completely comfortable with all this. She didn't squirm, she was totally relaxed. She was touching him and kissing him confidently. The two of them together looked just like I felt with Matt—comfortable.

She is so much more mature and experienced than I am. It's weird, but it seems like our friendship has gotten stronger since Greg kissed me at the rest stop. All the jealousy I used to feel has fallen away. I feel like we are all so connected now. I wonder if he told her before tonight?

Greg kissed me again, and then Samantha. Back and forth, back and forth, like a teeter totter of messed up.

Samantha leaned across him a little and held my hand as she kissed Greg.

At least if she is holding my hand, she's not putting it somewhere I don't want it to be.

Samantha had always told me she loved me and been super supportive of me in the gym, outwardly, but it wasn't until she told me her secret that I started to feel a real bond with her.

Maybe it was just how much attention Greg paid to me all this time? How does this experience make it better, though? This is out of control.

"My back is hurting. Will you adjust me?" Samantha asked Greg.

Hideaway beds aren't that comfortable, I thought. *At least this changes things up. I can take a deep breath and try to understand this.*

"Sure, come lay over here on the floor next to T," he said as he got up from the bed, walked around next to me, and then kneeled over her after she laid down. I heard the pop, pop, pop of her back being adjusted, while I squirmed again.

What now?

"Do you want a back massage, Samantha?" he asked.

"Sure," she answered. He was right next to me, kneeling over her. While his left hand was on her, his right hand was on my chest and he was leaning over me and kissing me again. I felt less comfortable all alone on the bed, but the next thing I knew he had pulled my shirt clear up and off.

"Can you work on my traps, T?" he asked, as he leaned over me to kiss me again.

"Sure," I was thankful to have something to do with my hands that didn't involve his penis. His lower body was clearly much closer to Samantha now, and that's where I wanted it.

As I grabbed the thick bulk of his left trapezius, he put his head down on my bare chest and started licking and nibbling my skin. He was kissing my breasts and sucking on my nipples, and my hormones were racing almost as fast as my heart. Greg was so big and he was leaning over on me like he was not quite in control of his body. Samantha was on floor next to me and she was clearly enjoying her "back massage."

I don't think she's just getting a back massage. I don't even want to know. Why is she making those noises?

I felt his body shudder as his lips were all over my chest sucking, nibbling, exploring; and while I felt dirty and wrong, I could feel arousal all over my body.

Matt is the only other person who has ever had my shirt off and made me feel this way, but with him it feels good and right. This just feels wrong, but I can't stop it. I can't just walk out. I love him. What would he and Samantha do if I got up and walked out? I can't do that. I am a part of this now too.

I just went with it, but I was exhausted.

What time is it? I shifted my body to a more comfortable position and tried to break the mood that was allowing this to go on.

Samantha was quieter now and maybe even asleep. Greg slowed down and rested his head on my chest.

"I love you, T."

"I love you, too." The words that I found so hard to utter just a few years prior poured out of me so easily now.

"I'm going to miss you more than anyone else." He wrapped both of his huge hands around my rib cage and squeezed. With his head and his two hands on me, almost all my skin was covered.

Samantha must be asleep, I thought.

"Sure you are. You've got a lot of people to miss, Greg."

"I do, but you're the one I count on. You're the one I confide in. You're the one I REALLY love," he whispered.

He hugged me tight and kissed me for a long time. "I've got to get some sleep and so do you. Samantha's sleeping already. Good night, T. Thanks for coming tonight."

I waited until he left the room and I got up and pulled my shirt back on. When I knew he was done in the bathroom, I went in and brushed my teeth and peed, noticing that my underwear was soaked.

Ugh. This is so wrong.

My mind was swimming. I didn't have a place in my brain to file this night or anything I was feeling.

He must love us so much to spend this time with us. He's right, he IS leaving his whole family – mom, dad, brothers. He is the one starting over completely, but he has also made himself SO MUCH to us, and in a lot of ways it's as if the last few years have all been leading to this. He asked us to talk to him. He wanted us to trust him and confide in him about our families and our boyfriends. He led us to lean on him and to need him. And now, he's leaving us.

I walked back to the living room, crawled under the covers, and tried to stop all the thoughts from ricocheting through my brain, so that I could finally go to sleep. I laid there staring at the little red lights of the stereo system in front of me.

Did all of that just happen? Not just tonight, but all of it? From the sexual innuendos, to the stories, to the rest stop, to the lake, to the freaking ménage e trois that just occurred? What WAS that?

The adrenaline must have finally worn off, and I must have fallen asleep, because the next thing I knew I was awake in the early morning. It must have been just after sunrise and neither Samantha nor Greg were up. Sometime in the night, Samantha had awakened and moved back into the bed next to me, but I hadn't heard her.

This was it—his last day of coaching our team. It was Saturday, and practice started at ten. I slowly rolled out of bed, trying not to disturb Samantha, grabbed my backpack and pulled out the book I was reading, *The Sun Also Rises*. It was on my summer reading list for Honors English, and I loved Hemingway. I opened it, happy to do summer homework, and tried to forget about the craziness that was last night.

It's just so wrong. How did I get myself into this? Tracy warned me. What the hell?

I lost myself in the story for an hour or so until I heard Greg moving.

How's this going to go?

He came out dressed for work in his typical YGC uniform. He gave me a hug, but no kiss.

"Want some pancakes?" he asked quietly.

"Sure."

Pancakes? Really?

I went to the bathroom and brushed my teeth.

Maybe he didn't kiss me because I haven't brushed my teeth.

I put on my black leotard and black shorts with a black tie-dyed T-shirt. This was a day of mourning and loss, so Samantha and I had decided to dress in black.

When Samantha woke up, Greg gave her a hug, and then we all sat there and ate pancakes together.

This is normal, right?

Samantha went to the bathroom and changed into her mourning outfit too.

"What's the plan for getting to the gym?" I hadn't been playing this sneaking around game long and I wasn't sure how they did it.

"I'll drop you two off on the cemetery side of the gym so you can go in without me. Let's go pretty soon, so that not everyone is there." Greg seemed super cool about the plan.

And that was it. We cleaned up the house, loaded into Greg's car, and went to our final practice with him as our coach.

No big deal.

Chapter Nine:
Declining at the Dance

Winter 1992

Let's just get this over with so I can get home and get ready for homecoming.

I couldn't have been more uncomfortable, sweating in my silk shirt and pants, shifting my weight from foot to foot in angst, wishing I were somewhere else.

"You may kiss the bride," the officiant nodded at my dad, who leaned in to kiss my new step-mom.

Gross.

I didn't like her. I was pissed that my dad sold my childhood home, and that my cat and our family dog had died when they decided to get married. Derek wasn't fond of her either, if for no other reason than she vacuumed the house three times a day, starting at 6 a.m.

I looked at Derek standing there in his multicolored silk shirt, pleated pants, and fluffy brown hair. He'd gotten taller and thinned out in the last few years. He wasn't my awkward, brace-faced, husky wearing, dorky brother anymore—he was a man. He shaved. He noticed me looking at him and wrinkled his nose at the situation at hand. I did a little eye roll back at him.

Thank God the ceremony is over! I'm going home as soon as humanly possible.

Derek and I hung out for a bit, quietly making snide

comments about our new stepfamily, until we both felt like we'd been there long enough.

"Dad, I'm going home. I have to get ready for the dance and Derek has plans, so he's leaving too. Love you." I gave my dad a hug goodbye, hoping this day would not be a huge regret for him.

I wish he'd signed a pre-nup.

Derek had his usual weekend plans with his guys—cruising the strip in Salem between Burger Chef and McDonald's in their muscle cars and drinking Miller Lite. He had just turned eighteen and was heading into his senior year.

He seems too old for high school, I thought as I waved goodbye to him and pulled out of the driveway. I had just gotten my license and loved every chance to drive the blue Geo Prism hatchback, even if it was my mom's and even if it was another grey Ohio day.

Someday I'll live at the beach. I'd live on the Outer Banks in Hatteras, North Carolina in a heartbeat.

Thirty minutes later, I pulled into my driveway, hopped out of the car, and scrambled up the stairs. I still had a few hours before I needed to get ready for the dance and meet Matt at his house for pictures.

Ugh...a dance. Dressing up.

I collapsed onto my bed and stared at the black velvet dress with the huge purple iridescent bow on the back, hanging on my closet door. It wasn't really my style, but then again, dresses weren't my style. It was what I bought with Mom, so it'd have to do.

I don't feel beautiful enough for a dance. Shit, I don't even feel cute. I feel like shit.

Lying on my white, metal-framed daybed, I heard a very soft rain starting to fall.

Great, my hair's going to look like shit too.

There was an eave in my room and the ceilings were low. It felt kind of like a cave in there, which I loved. I was up on the second story, so I could look out at the trees. Most of my walls were coated with pictures of River Phoenix, Johnny Depp, the

Coreys (Haim and Feldman), Kirk Cameron, Leonardo DiCaprio, and Patrick Swayze. No New Kids on the Block for me, thanks.

I could just go to sleep right now, I thought, as my eyelids seemed to close involuntarily. *No, I don't have time to sleep. I do have time to read them again though...*

I pushed off my stomach, up onto my elbows. I reached under my mattress and pulled out the letters. The paper was neat and clean, and there was his crazy handwriting. The letters always came in the same sized envelope; some of them had his name and return address, and some didn't. They were a touchstone for my sanity (or maybe insanity) and I had probably read them at least twenty times. The first one was my favorite.

Dear Honey, Baby, Sugar, Lovey Dovey, Sunshine of my existence, Sweetheart Petunia, (Laying it on a little thick, eh?)

As you know, #1. I do not have INXS's new tape.

#2. You can usually call me between 7:35 and 8:00pm your time. Marylou is usually, no promises, not home then. Call Monday through Friday. (what you didn't know)

#3. Yes. I love you a lot. More than a lot, you are the queen of my heart, queen of hearts, especially mine. (what you should always know)

Now, we need to talk about me and Samantha. I don't really know what happened with me and Samantha. She was going through a tough time with school, her parents, and gymnastics. We started having little talks and after while (months) she kissed me, as I hugged her goodbye.

From then on I felt obligated to return her affection and

physical advances. It seemed like I was always lifting her and supporting her, and she did little or nothing for me. That night at my house it might have seemed like more from my part, but that was a crazy night for me. That night I just went nuts. Ok. All the details of that night still aren't clear. Obviously, all the time and effort I put in with Samantha kept her in the sport (gymnastics) and helped her self-esteem and get over family problems. I knew it wasn't the right way to do that, but it was what I did with the short time I had available with her. I know it sounds weird, but I know that you'll understand it also. It's also pretty apparent that Samantha was always thinking about Samantha. It's apparent that true emotions weren't involved. Look at how many times she's written me since I've been here. One time in two months. Samantha took what Samantha wanted kind of using me as a crutch. Now that she's healed she doesn't seem to need the crutch anymore. Get it? She got what she needed from me at the time: love, caring and understanding. And now that I am not there to give her that constantly she has kind of forgot about me. A little selfish, don't you think? I wish the physical things didn't happen between me and her, but they did and I'm sorry. I don't think we had a strong mental bond (real love) because I was the one that was always giving and giving and giving. Mainly, she just took what I had to offer her and didn't give much back. Now, I want you to know about you and I:

#1 Do we still have a mental and emotional relationship

even though we're separated by distance?

#2 Do we still show care and concern for each other?

#3 Was our relationship ever based only on physical actions? (I dream about it.)

#4 Do you feel a bond (real love) for me?

#5 Do you feel like you can tell me anything?

#6 If you could would you marry me? (Just joking)

#7 Did (do) you enjoy just being near me?

#8 Do you feel good (great) when you think about me?

#9 Do you think about me often?

#10 Do you wish I was your constant companion?

If you answered yes to most (or all of them like I did) of these questions then our relationship is way better and way more than anything Samantha and I ever had. I never discussed my problems with Marylou or anything else unless it was with you or you were around. Samantha was only concerned about her problems. I love you. I told you years ago, you were on the beam, that you are the best person I know to talk to. You can be reasoned with and have a lot of understanding. Do you remember that? Over the years you have gotten more wonderful. Remember, <u>I kissed you</u>. That was a crazy day. Even that night I can remember being with you more than Samantha. I love you. You are great. Enough of that...

The letter went on, but that first part was the best part, the part that allowed me to breathe, and feel like I wasn't completely insane or a horrible person. I was okay. He loved me. In fact, he loved me more. The end was good too:

...I hope you understand how I feel about you a little better. I love you.

Love,

Greg

P.S. I miss you. Try to destroy this highly incriminating letter. XXOO

Ugh...I miss him so much.
I read the first part of the letter again.
Since Greg left, I felt like someone had died. I'd stayed at the gym until we went to Spain for the World's Fair, and then I quit gymnastics for good just before school started this year.
I can't believe I'm only a junior. I'm so ready to be out of high school.
No more long, hot, painful practices. No more ankle and back pain. No more tears in the gym. No more teammates to compete against and lean on. No more gymnastics. No more Greg.
He was adamant about us writing to him, and I liked to write anyway, so I started the day he left and had probably sent him ten letters in just a few months. This was the first letter I got from him, and I read it often.
It's so good to know that he loved me more than her. I was

and still am special to him.

I folded the letter up and put it back under my mattress with the two others, sighing out loud as I stood up and walked over to the dress.

I'd decided to wear my hair down because it was long and Matt liked it down. As I went to work with the curling iron (which was hopeless really because it was raining), I glanced down at my body.

God, I feel gross. I'm not pretty. I'm losing my muscles.

I may have gained a few pounds since quitting gymnastics, but it was more than that.

I feel dirty. I know Greg loves me and he cares about me and I'm special to him, but I still cheated on Matt. And Greg cheated on Marylou with not only me, but Samantha too.

Fixing the last curl, I turned my attention to makeup and my mind drifted to how Matt and I hadn't been getting along as well as we used to. Lately, it seemed like we fought a lot and couldn't agree on anything.

Tonight will be good for us. We'll have fun together, I thought as I brushed the mascara onto my lashes. *I feel frustrated, but I can't imagine not being with him. I love him so much. He's the best guy ever, and I totally love him. But, at the same time, something's not right with us.*

The week before, someone had asked me if Matt was dating another girl at our school and I laughed it off, thinking they weren't serious, until I saw they were.

"No, because we're still dating," I'd said with more confidence than I felt. I knew she and Matt were friends and had several classes together, but that was kind of weird, so I had asked him about it.

"We're just friends. I have a lot of classes with her," he'd said. That was all I needed to hear.

I trust him. I know he loves me. I'm not threatened by her. Not everyone cheats.

I finished the last swipe of mascara and nodded at myself in the mirror.

You look alright. Maybe you'll have a good night. I think this love will last, unlike my parents. What would my life be like if it had just stayed the four of us—Mom, Dad, Derek and me, on Route 45 in Salem forever? I wouldn't have met Matt. What if Greg hadn't crossed that line with me? What if love actually lasted?

I pulled on my purple panty hose, zipped up my dress, donned some earrings and my black high heels, and carefully walked down the stairs, determined to make the best of the night.

Tight dresses and high heels are not my comfort zone.

Mom called to me from the back deck when she heard my heels clicking in the kitchen, "Are you ready to go, Honey?"

"Yeah, I guess," I said flatly, wishing I felt happy and excited.

She came in the house and her eyes lit up. "You look amazing, Torey."

"Thanks, Mom," I said with more enthusiasm than I felt as I gave her a hug.

Mom is sweet. Thank God she doesn't know the truth about all the shit I have done.

Mom drove me to Matt's house and came in to take some pictures.

I feel like I am at a funeral again.

I glanced up at Matt, who was sporting a small cold sore and wasn't quite his normal "hotter than hot" self that night. He was six inches taller than me, with the brightest blue eyes you've ever seen, light brown hair, and soft skin over a perfectly muscular seventeen-year-old body. HOT. Smart, funny, sweet, and always up for an adventure, he was the love of my life ever since we met in that damn eighth grade English class when I couldn't stop crying. We'd been dating for about a year and half, but he'd been on my radar for four years. He was the one.

I feel broken. I feel like we are falling apart. I should be happy and excited for Homecoming. Why do I feel so gross?

"Send me lovely pictures. The kind I'll really like." Greg's words out of one of his last letters danced through my mind,

appearing to answer my question.

I can't imagine taking naked pictures, but I know that's what he means.

I'd barely been naked with Matt, and when that had happened, it was dark. There were people in our class that got together and played strip poker, and it made me so uncomfortable that I always found a way to avoid it.

How can I be such a prude and yet feel so dirty?

More memories flooded my mind. That time when Greg was adjusting my back, and asked me if I had put my mouth on Matt. And then, the letter he wrote, asking me to put my lips on a circle that was drawn at the top of the page and mail it back to him.

Gross, why did I do it? He's three states away, and still SO in my head. It's like I can't say NO.

"Tor, you ready?" Matt held out his hand and nodded toward the door.

God, he's hot, even with a cold sore, I thought, but then that sick feeling of knowing I had wronged him overwhelmed me.

"Yes, let's go." I smiled a fake smile and we left to the dance.

When we arrived, I offered the same fake smile and hugs to my friends and acted like a "normal teenager," but I felt dead inside.

Shouldn't this be a great night with Matt and my friends? I chided myself as we moved toward the dance floor. *I just want to get into the dark again, so I don't have to smile that smile that I have to force, that I don't feel in my heart.*

Matt had his arm around my *waste* (I mean *waist*) when "Wonderful Tonight" by Eric Clapton started playing. This was our song, and I sort of collapsed onto his shoulder.

"What's wrong?" he asked. "Was it your dad's wedding?"

"I don't know, Matt. I just don't feel like being here. I'd rather be home with you in your room."

Matt started singing in my ear, trying to help me relax and enjoy the night:

"It's late in the evening; she's wondering what

clothes to wear.

She puts on her makeup, and brushes her long blond hair

And then she asks me, Do I look alright?

And I say yes, you look wonderful tonight."

"You do look amazing," he said with his "serious" look. We goofed around a lot together, but I always knew when he was being sincere.

What a good guy.

"Thanks. I love you. You look great, too. I think I'm just tired. I don't really give a shit that my Dad got married. It just sucks that he sold our old house. It's like nothing of my childhood is left."

"Yeah, I get it. I mean, I don't really get it, because my parents are still together, and I've never moved, but I've seen how all this has affected you. You're strong, Torey, but this shit isn't easy." He nuzzled my cheek and held me tighter. I could feel the strength of his arms around me and the absolute comfort of being with him rushed through me.

I love the feel of his muscles, I thought as I ran my fingers down his back.

"Thanks, Matt, I don't know what I'd do without you. I know I haven't been the best girlfriend lately, and it sort of shook me when someone asked me if you were dating someone else. I know we've been arguing a lot and I'm sorry. I'll try to be better for you. I'll try to be happier," I promised as I put my head on his shoulder, but I wasn't sure quite how to do that.

"I love you, Torey. We'll be okay." He pulled me even closer and put his head in my neck while we danced.

As my body swayed back and forth on the dance floor, my mind was like a pinball machine: *I feel so guilty about what happened with Greg, but I can't tell anyone. No one would understand. I feel like shit about cheating on Matt. He deserves better. I did this. I brought this on myself. I could have stopped it and I didn't. I wanted to be special to Greg and instead I'm messing this up with Matt. God, I hope he's right about us being okay.*

My dress was so tight that it made the perfect excuse for not fast dancing. I tolerated the dance for an hour or two, and then Matt and I said our goodbyes and left. He had brought a change of clothes, and I was eager to get out of the confines of the fitted dress and heels, so we went by my house to change and then got back in his car.

It was a pretty warm fall night and no longer raining. Matt looked over at me with a question, "Voc?" and I smiled. The vocational school was where we went to just lay under the stars and listen to frogs. We just cuddled and enjoyed being outside and away from parents. Matt and I had our best conversations outside, and I was happy we'd have a few hours to lay quietly in the dark together.

He backed out of my driveway and drove the few minutes to the "Voc" with the Doors' "Light My Fire" blaring and the windows down.

THIS is my style.

He pulled into a parking spot in the back, where the cops wouldn't see his car unless they pulled clear into the lot. He got out and grabbed a thick flannel blanket and some snacks from the trunk. I grabbed my hooded sweatshirt for a little more warmth, and we held hands as we walked back through the dewy grass to our spot.

I leaned over, put my head on his shoulder, and said, "I love you," and he kissed the top of my head and whispered, "I love you, too."

He laid the blanket down and sat down while I was looking up at the stars and listening to the few frogs that were still braving the fall weather. When I glanced down at him, he patted the spot next to him. I took a deep breath, sat down, and snuggled up next to him.

"What's going on in your head, Tor?" he asked, as he put his arm around me and pulled me to lay back with him.

Tears welled up almost immediately as I laid my head on his shoulder.

I'm SO GLAD it's dark.

"I don't know, Matt. I'm just not happy," I confessed as tears rolled down my cheeks. "It doesn't have anything to do with you. It's not us that's wrong; it's me. Maybe it's just gymnastics being over. It was such a huge part of my life, but I just don't feel great about anything in my life right now." It was painful to even say the words because I knew they would hurt him, but I couldn't lie to him.

What's wrong with me? Why am I not happy?

"Well that's hard not to take personally. I would hope I'd be a pretty big part of your life; you are a huge part of mine." He looked into my eyes with puppy dog sadness.

"I know, I know. You're amazing and I don't know how else to explain that it's nothing to do with you. I've never been as happy as I was when we first started dating, and there's no one else I can imagine being with, but there's something that's not right with *me*." I took a deep breath, looked up at the stars and noticed Orion's belt.

Seriously, what's wrong with me? I have this incredible guy who I was in love with for two years before we started dating. I have what I want, right here! I DON'T have an eating disorder. We have enough money. Both my parents are alive and well. I know tons of people who are way worse off than I am. Why can't I just be happy?

"Well, what do we need to do?" he asked as he pulled me in close and kissed me.

"That's a good start," I murmured when we came up for air.

Matt was never pushy, and while we had been intimate in the past, he never expected anything of me and was good at reading what I was comfortable with. He kissed me again, and hugged me tight.

"Let's just lay here and look at the stars together for a while. Sometimes maybe we just need a little space and time," he suggested with a squeeze.

"Thanks. That sounds good, but you can still kiss me if you want." I smiled and leaned over him. He smiled back, then grabbed me and steam rolled over me to the other side of the blanket.

I love how playful he is.

"You know there is no one I would have rather spent tonight with, right? Happy or unhappy."

"I think I know that. We'll be okay, Matt. I think I just need some time to get used to all this change." I looked up at the stars and immersed myself in the warmth and comfort of just being there next to him.

It's so good to have someone who loves me for me and who doesn't ask much of me.

"Shooting star!" We both saw it at the same time.

"Make a wish," I said, as I closed my eyes and thought, *I wish I could feel happy, whole, and good again. I wish I would never have let anything happen with Greg. I wish I were a better girlfriend.*

It was getting late when Matt checked the time. "We have to get you home," he said.

"Ugh. Can't we just stay here, together, forever?" I groaned as I pulled myself up off his shoulder.

"Not yet, Babe, but maybe someday. C'mon." He grabbed my hand and pulled me up, then folded the blanket while I grabbed all our stuff. We walked back to his car hand in hand. He opened the door for me and I dropped into the bucket seat.

Such a gentleman, I love those little things he does. I love his poetry, and his little notes to me.

We drove the few minutes back to my house as we listened to The Doors' "The Crystal Ship" with a little less volume this time, and I held his free hand.

This guy is so awesome. He's the only good thing in my life right now. I'm so lucky to have him.

As he pulled into my driveway and turned off the car, we could see the light on in the living room.

"Susie's up," he said with a smile and a twinkle in his eye.

That mischievous twinkle is the first thing I ever noticed about this boy.

"Yep, probably waiting for the full report. I haven't talked to her about the wedding yet, so that should be fun."

Matt got out, and walked around to open my door.

Gentleman.

He held my hand as we walked to the front door. "I love you, Torey, and I want you to be happy."

"I love you too, Matthew Connor," I said with a smile, "and, I am working on it. Thanks for tonight. I loved the 'voc' as much as the dance. You're the best." I kissed him goodbye and watched him walk back to his blue Honda, where he blew me a kiss before getting in the car.

I waited until he had pulled out of the driveway, and then quietly opened the front door. The light was on, but Mom wasn't around, so she must have just left it on for me.

Thank goodness. I have no desire to talk to her. I clicked off the light and went upstairs as quietly as I could. I skipped teeth brushing and face washing and just crawled into bed, where I could escape my brain until tomorrow. As I lay there waiting for sleep, I could feel the letters beneath me like the pea under the princess.

Chapter Ten:
Collapse at College

Fall 1994

It was a crisp fall day at The Ohio State University, and now Matt and I were both freshmen at OSU; but we had stopped dating shortly after that homecoming dance. It was as if we just disintegrated. The last year and half of high school was hard because I couldn't get away from him, but here at OSU there were fifty thousand undergraduates for me to lose myself among. I missed Matt, but it was more the purity and innocence of our relationship that I really missed. That was gone.

I was reading some Philosophy notes when the phone in my dorm rang. I jumped up from my bed and picked up the phone that hung on the wall.

"Hello?" I answered, happy for an excuse to stop reading on a Friday afternoon.

"Hi, is Torey there?" a male voice asked.

"This is she," I said politely.

I don't recognize this voice.

"Hi Torey, this is Samantha's boyfriend. I'm having a party tonight and wondered if you would come to surprise her?"

Oh yeah! Samantha's Ohio State boyfriend!

"Hi. Yes, I'd love to see her! Thanks for calling. Where do you live?"

How cool that he thought to call me.

107

"Great! It's on 9th St, pretty close to Neil Avenue. You won't miss it if you head in that direction. Oh, and Torey, don't be afraid to bring your girlfriends. We'll have at least ten kegs."

"Awesome. Thanks. That sounds great. I should be able to convince my girls to make the trek to South Campus for that many kegs. I'll try to bring a few."

"Alright, well then, I'll see you tonight!"

"Cool. See you later." I hung up the phone, crashed back onto my bed, and started thinking.

Sweet, ten keg party means we aren't paying to drink tonight.

My girls were Lindsay, Sarah, and Beth, and they lived in the same dorm as I did, the nerd dorm of North Campus. Our other plans would not have provided beer, so it was a safe bet we would head to South Campus.

I'll get to see Samantha!

I had only seen her a handful of times since quitting gymnastics, and not for at least a year. I hadn't even made it to any of her college gymnastics meets yet.

It'll be good to see her.

I picked up the phone and called downstairs to the girls to let them know. Linds picked up. "Hello?"

"Hey, it's Torey."

"Hi, Tors!" Linds said happily.

"Hey! I just got the invite to a ten kegger on South Campus tonight. Are you in?"

"Sure. Can I invite my roommates?"

"Of course! And it's noodles for dinner tonight, so do you want to do Adriatico's instead?" I knew she hated the noodles.

"Definitely." I could hear her scowl. "Want to meet in our room at seven?"

"That sounds good, see you in a few hours."

"Ok, later Tors," Linds said as she hung up the phone.

I'm super lucky to have her as a friend. She's the shit.

I headed back to my bedroom to try to read a bit more. My roommate was gone for the weekend and it was almost too quiet in there. I lit some incense and flipped through my CD case. INXS, U2, Gin Blossoms, Sublime, Bob Marley, Cat Stevens, Led Zeppelin, Talking Heads, Dave Matthews Band, Mother Love Bone, Seven Mary Three, Blues Traveler, REM, The Eagles, Beastie Boys, Alice in Chains, Stone Temple Pilots, Dead Poets soundtrack...

I love my music.

I pulled out Pearl Jam, *Ten,* and put it in my 6-disc changer and hit play. This album reminded me of riding around in the back of a car at night with Samantha and some of her friends a few years ago, not long after I quit gymnastics.

It's going to be good to see her. I wonder how she is? I wonder if she's still in love with Greg?

I looked at the reading that I wanted to do for a while, but as I laid there staring at it, my mind kept going back to that night that Samantha and I had spent with Greg at his house.

I wonder how she feels about that now? I wonder if she still writes to him, like I do?

The letters he wrote me had become mostly about his family and school now, but Greg and I were still in touch every few months.

I still love him, and now it's more platonic and good again, I thought, as "Jeremy" played. *I hope Samantha has found that with him too, and I hope we can have fun like we used to.*

It was obviously useless to continue to read on a Friday afternoon, so I jumped in the shower and got dressed to go out for the night. Clean jeans, a t-shirt, black Pumas, and my classic Ohio State sweatshirt. I'd be comfortable and warm enough, especially if I was drinking lots of beer, which was standard. I put on some eyeliner and got my MILK (money, ID, lipstick, keys) together. I glanced at the clock, it was only 6:30 p.m., but I hadn't seen my guy friends all day, so I headed downstairs to their room.

I'll stop in and see them before I head to Linds's room.

I walked down my hall to the stairs, down a flight and back to almost directly below my own room. I knocked on the door and, without waiting, opened it. These guys all felt like brothers to me. I hung out with them as much, if not more, than Linds and the girls. They were all smart and they all happened to be fairly cool (not the norm in the Honors dorm).

I hung out there often and sometimes 'til the wee hours of the morning, but I didn't date any of them.

Platonic, good, safe.

I got burned early on first quarter by a guy a few years older and "wiser". He was the first guy who cheated on me and broke up with me. It had hit me hard, and my guard was up when it came to a relationship or a commitment.

Whatever. Alcoholic, cigarette-smoking dick. Why did I fall for a guy like that? Why can't I want to date one of these guys who would be so much better for me? They feel like brothers—that's why. Or, maybe I don't deserve them. They are GOOD guys.

"Hi, guys!" I said as I walked in the door.

"Hi! Hey!" they said almost simultaneously. I was like an annoying sister to these guys, and I loved it.

"Votaw!" Brad said with his usual playfulness.

Brad was in a heated Tetris battle.. The pieces were falling as fast as the letters on the computer screens in the movie, "The Matrix."

I don't know how these guys play like this!

I never liked hanging out with them when they were playing video games.

Not my scene.

They were ridiculously competitive and way too good at video games for anyone who has a life in the real world. Their room was clean compared to most guys' dorm rooms. Four Type A overachiever boys living together in one small space, *interesting.*

Crazy boys.

I sat and watched the battle for a few minutes, and then I asked, "What's on the agenda tonight?"

"You're lookin' at it!" Brad replied without missing a beat or moving his eyes from the screen. "It's an all-night Tetris-a-thon."

"Seriously? Ugh. How are you guys ever going to meet girls

if you stay in your rooms playing video games on Friday nights?"

"Don't worry, Votaw, there'll be girls. Some little friends from high school are coming in an hour or so," Brad said with a mischievous grin and a twinkle in his bright blue eyes.

"Um, creepy!" I said with a motherly tone. "Well, have fun with that, kids. I'll see you tomorrow. Wanna grab breakfast?" I asked as I headed towards the door.

"Sounds good. Meet here at nine," Brad said, but his eyes didn't leave the screen.

"Wait, what are you up to tonight, Votaw?" Brad asked, just as I was walking out.

"Ten keg party on South Campus," I said with a smile.
Girls always drink for free.

"Damn you, Votaw!" Brad shot back.

"Back at ya, Brad! Have fun with Tetris and the high school girls, boys!"

I love those guys, I thought, as I walked out and headed down the stairs to floor three again. *Why can't I fall in love with a good guy like Brad?*

Linds and Sarah were ready to go.

"We've been calling you. We're starving! Let's go!" Sarah said. With her full cheeks and straight brown hair, Sarah was about my height and just huggable. She was so laid back and sweet, yet smart as a whip and funny too. She was the quiet napping type, always a bit reserved and seemingly sleepy, but a super hard worker and loyal friend.

"I was in 814, but yes! Adriatico's, here we come. Where's Beth?" I asked.

"She's hanging with her sister tonight. She doesn't want her corrupted, so they took the bus to a movie," Linds said with a hint of indignation. Linds was a few inches taller than me, with pouty beautiful lips and naturally curly short brown hair. She was thin but had huge boobs.

Not fair, I thought as she pulled on her jacket.

"Okay, well then, let's go." I locked arms with Linds and started skipping.

Friday night on campus!!

We headed out and started walking toward Adriatico's, the best pizza place on South Campus. It was just so good. The dough was an inch thick, and the pizzas were rectangular instead of circular. The sauce was just a little spicy, and each square piece had a three-inch in diameter piece of pepperoni on it.

I LOVE this pizza.

The three of us shared a medium and were all stuffed. We drank as much pop as we could in the hopes of it helping us stay up longer and stomach more beer. Sarah and Linds could both drink as much beer, if not more, than I could. Not that we were officially keeping track, but drinking was a thing at Ohio State. It was something we did. We drank. A LOT. The guys in our circle had a case club and the girls had a 12-pack club. I was not in it, though I may have made it to 11 once.

We finished up dinner and headed out toward the party. It was dark already, and the fall night was clear and brisk. Music emanated from all directions, some louder than others, and there were students walking intently from place to place. Some were laughing and kidding around, some solo headed to study and, of course, some couples snuggled up and holding hands.

How do they make that happen? I haven't had a good relationship since Matt and I broke up. Why am I so bad at this?

Sarah's question got me out of my head.

"Who do you know here, Torey?" she asked with questioning eyes.

"It's my friend Samantha's boyfriend's house. She goes to Bowling Green, she's a gymnast and a year ahead of us, but her boyfriend is here. I think I've only met him once. They are both from close to my home, but more out in the country. You know, guys that bale hay have the best arms!" I said with a twinkle in my eye.

"You're hilarious, Tors." Linds said with her funny-to-me, central Ohio drawl. "What do you know about guys that bale hay? You grew up in the suburbs!"

"Yeah, but I was born in farmland where there was plenty of

hay, as well as boys who bailed it. Their arms are so nice. I'm just saying, there should be some older hottie boys there, I hope, and plenty of booze."

"Always a good start to a party," Sarah nodded in agreement.

We walked toward the corner address, and it was obvious from a few blocks away that we were headed in the right direction. By the time we got close it was obvious they had tapped the kegs a few hours before, based on the amount of people and the state of them. The music was loud, and we made our way to the kegs and got ourselves a beer. I asked around for Samantha or her boyfriend, but no one seemed to know where they were. No one ever minded girls showing up, so we made ourselves at home and filled our cups. As I got out of the keg line, I saw that Linds and Sarah were already in a conversation with some guys.

"I'm going inside to find Samantha," I yelled to them over the Beastie Boys "Watcha, watcha, watcha want" that was blaring. They raised their cups at me and nodded. I trusted they would be fine, and went inside, beer in hand.

I saw a few people from Samantha's high school that I recognized, and I asked about her again. One person thought she was upstairs, but he wasn't sure.

"I'll go look," he offered and walked away.

I hung out with the people I sort of knew and finished my first beer. When it had been longer than I thought it should take, I said, "I'm going to go grab another beer and check on my friends. Let Samantha know I'll be right back if you see her?"

They nodded to me as I headed outside. The music was so loud no one could really hear anything, and it was hard to make conversation with people I didn't know that well.

This is kind of awkward, but I want to see Samantha.

I made my way back outside into the chilly night air and looked for Sarah and Linds.

I love that fall smell. I love Ohio State.

I saw them across the deck, still in conversation and seeming quite content. I waved, refilled my cup, and then headed back inside.

As I made it inside, I saw Samantha and her boyfriend coming down the steps. I waved and she ran up to me and picked me up in a big strong bear hug. She looked amazing, just like she always had. Her eyes were bright. Her jeans were tight, so you could see her muscular legs under them, and her short-sleeved shirt showed off her biceps. She was the picture of health. We immediately embraced and were dancing around in a circle but in a tight hug.

Wow, it's so good to see her.

"How ARE you? It's so good to see you!" Her smile spread across her face.

"I'm good. SO glad to be out of Youngstown, and on my own here! How are you? How's gymnastics?" I asked, wanting to know everything at once.

She looks amazing. She must have her shit totally together.

"Good, good. I can barely hear you. Let me get a beer and then let's go upstairs where we can talk." She grabbed my hand, and we walked outside to the tapped keg. She filled her mug, and I dragged her over to introduce her to Linds and Sarah. I could tell they were buzzed by the size of their smiles and the proximity of the guys they were talking to. They said a quick hello, and I told them we are going upstairs to hang out if they needed me. Hand in hand, Samantha and I walked back through the thumping music and smells of beer and incense to her boyfriend's bedroom.

When we got inside where it was quieter, I asked again, "How's gymnastics going, super college athlete, friend?"

She was still holding my hand, and we were sitting on the bed. It was so much quieter in his room, even with the blaring Sublime emanating from downstairs, "I don't practice Santeria, I ain't got no crystal ball…" The room was coated in Ohio State and psychedelic black light posters. There was a lava lamp, a pile of books on the desk, and a guitar in the corner.

I could be in just about any OSU undergrad's room.

"It's great! It's so much different than club gymnastics in

114

high school. I feel like my teammates are my sisters and we're all in it together. It's kind of like once you get that scholarship, the competition factor subsides and we're really all part of a team. I love it, and my coach is amazing."

"Good for you. I have heard you are kicking some ass. How's your boyfriend? You guys have been dating for a while now, right?" I took a big swig of my beer, feeling a little buzzed and happy to be with my old friend, wondering how she had it all together.

How can she have this successful relationship, and this amazing life after all that went on for her? What happened with me was no big deal compared to what Greg did with her.

"Yeah, two years now." She smiled.

"Awesome. That's a long time. Are you going to marry him?" I asked, winking at her. It felt like we could easily start where we had left off, and my style was never to chit chat about nothing anyway.

She laughed and laid back on his bed, "God, Torey, I don't know. I still can't stop thinking about you know who."

"Greg? Really?" I asked, my voice cracking a bit with his name.

Wow. So, it is still a thing for her.

"Yeah. I don't know if I'll ever feel like that again. I don't love him like I loved Greg."

"But, Samantha, that wasn't good, right? I mean, if he loved you, why did he marry Marylou? And, if he loved you, why did he kiss me?"

Tears welled up in her eyes and I could tell my mere presence, as well as my forthright questions, were bringing back a lot of memories for her.

"I know you are right in my head, but my heart just can't let go of him." The tears began to stream down her face.

God, that sucks for her.

"Have you talked to him?" I asked, taking the pulse on where their relationship had gone and another swig of my beer.

This is a dicey topic and I'd rather not feel anything. More

115

beer, more beer.

"Not much. I wrote him a few letters. He wrote me once or twice since he left, but nothing since the time we met him at your house."

My mind flashed back to Samantha and I walking with Greg and his three-year-old son, Daniel, a few years ago at my parent's house. It was a year or so after he had left Ohio, and he told us both that he was sorry about what happened with us. He said he had told Marylou and someone at his church what he had done, and was getting help. I trusted he was being honest, and I hugged him goodbye before he left. Samantha, on the other hand, told him she never wanted to talk to him again and walked back into my house.

She's so strong. Maybe I should have done that too.

Samantha's voice brought me back to the room. "What about you? Do you talk to him?" Tears pouring down her cheeks, she was still holding my hand as if she needed me to stay there with her and talk about this.

Talking about what happened makes it real. Otherwise it might disappear.

"Yeah, here and there. We were always more friends than anything else," I said. "I don't think I miss him like you do at all. I mean, I loved him, but not like you did."

"So, you don't think about him? You don't wish you were with him?" she asked with a catch in her throat.

"No, not like that. I mean, I reach out to him for advice on school and family stuff and maybe guys, but I don't wish I was WITH him," I said as honestly as I could.

I really wished that nothing had ever happened with us.

Oh my God, this sucks for her. I can't believe it's been over two years and she's still all wrapped up in Greg. How can she look so good and be so perfect on the outside, and have all this on the inside?

"Does your boyfriend know?" I asked, wondering how she deals with it.

"No. I still haven't told many people. Have you told

anyone?" There were so many more questions in her eyes.

"Not really. It all just makes me feel dirty, sad, and ashamed. I still don't understand it. Even after he explained it in some letters and apologized, I don't feel like it's okay. I mean, I KNEW about you. So, I was betraying you, my friend, AND I was cheating on Matt. And, Greg was cheating on his wife. AND, he was fifteen years older than me. How much more messed up can one situation be? It's just gross when I think back on it. Why did I let it happen? But somehow, I still love him."

My stomach was starting to hurt and I hated to see how upset Samantha was.

Damn, I'm going to need more beer for this conversation.

"Yeah, I don't know. I try to hate him, but the reality is, I can't stop thinking about him. How is Matt?"

"He's here at Ohio State. I barely see him, but when I do, it's like he's a totally different person. We broke up not long after Greg left, and he was with some girl he said was just a friend almost immediately after. That was a total dick move, and I don't think I'll ever forgive him. I loathed the two of them through the rest of high school because they were constantly all over each other in front of me, no matter which way I turned." I sighed and took another long pull from my beer.

My beer is almost gone. This is not what I was expecting tonight to be. This is hard. I feel so broken.

"Matt was a good guy, Torey. You guys were just young." She said it with a knowingness that I appreciated. She was a year older than me and had been a mentor in a lot of ways until she had gone off to college.

"Yeah, I know, but he doesn't seem like such a good guy now. I don't even know what I am looking for. I have great friends who are guys, but I am not attracted to them at all. I'm attracted to alcoholic assholes that cheat on me. How is it that you can date a guy for two years? How are you two?" I hoped she might have some magic answer.

"Well, it probably helps that I am doing gymnastics and constantly training or competing. I don't have time to visit too often, and he has a job so he doesn't come up to Bowling Green too much. I think we're good, but I don't think we are getting married anytime soon and…" Tears were pouring down her cheeks again. "I just feel like I'll never love anyone the way I loved Greg. Maybe I should have married him. Maybe I should have let him wait for me. Maybe then nothing would have happened with you, and he wouldn't have cheated on Marylou with us both, because he and I would have been together. I should not have let him involve you like he did. I could have stopped it."

Holy shit. That's a lot to carry. My stomach hurts. Why did I ever let myself get involved in all of this? I could have told someone. I could have stopped it for her.

"I don't know, Samantha, even though he only really kissed me a few times before he left, he had been talking about sex with me for years." Tears were streaming down my cheeks now, too. "I don't think you could have stopped it. And, do you really think he would have waited for you and married you?" I wanted so badly to have answers that would somehow make this okay.

"I don't know," she sputtered with sobs and snot.

There was a knock on the door, and as it opened, Nine Inch Nails came pouring in with the smell of cigarettes as her boyfriend came in. He was taken aback by the somber mood, and shut the door behind him before walking over to Samantha. She crumpled into his arms and was full body sobbing now.

I imagine there's going to a be a big conversation between these two tonight. What the hell do I do now?

I wiped my tears and said, "I'm going to go check on my friends and refill my beer. You guys take some time and I'll be back in a few." I was shaking as I walked down the stairs. The music was pounding, which made it easier to ignore the feelings brewing up inside me. "I want to f*** you like an animal, I want to feel you from the inside…" Trent Reznor's lyrics poured into my head as I thought, *I haven't thought or talked about the Greg situation to that length ever, with anyone, even Samantha. I read the letters a lot, and I think I have it clear in my head, but seeing how these memories affect Samantha, this is crazy. I need to just* *leave her alone. She's better off without me in her life.*

I found Linds and Sarah, and they were obviously ready to
go. "Where have you been all this time, Tors? Are you okay?"
Linds asked seeing the redness in my eyes.

"I was upstairs talking to Samantha," I said with a little
stutter.

*Get it together, Torey. Your story is nothing compared to
Samantha's. You can't just leave her up there in this state.*

"I need five minutes to say goodbye to her," I said as I filled
my cup at the keg again. "I'll be right back down." They rolled
their eyes at me and gave me the "get on with it already" look, but
I could tell they were also concerned.

I made my way back through the party, with a nauseous
feeling in my stomach and a heavy weight in my chest.

*Are we both totally messed up over this? It's gotta be SO
much worse for her. She was sleeping with him and in love with
him, and all we did was kiss and make out a little. What happened
with me was no big deal compared to what happened with her. The
best thing I can do is leave her alone. I bring back shit memories
for her, and I need to just stay away.*

I knocked lightly on the door and slid into the room.
Samantha was curled up in a ball by the closet and her boyfriend
was looking worried and confused sitting a few feet away from
her.

"She won't let me touch her. What the hell did you two talk
about?" he asked with a concerned and confused look.

"It's a long story, but she needs to be the one to tell you." I
spoke softly and walked over to her. She let me hug her, but didn't
say anything, just sobbed and turned away from me. There was a
blankness in her eyes, and I didn't know what else I could do but
leave.

*I brought this on. She'd be having fun at her boyfriend's keg
party if I hadn't shown up. I shouldn't have talked about it.*

"Samantha, I love you. I have to go."

She pulled me in a little tighter, and then let go. I kissed her
head, stood up, and practically ran back out to Linds and Sarah as I

tried to keep the tears back.

"Let's go," I said as I approached them, and we all started walking north.

It was about a mile or more back to the opposite corner of North Campus, and the night was cold so we were walking fast.

"Did you two have fun?" I asked with a wavering voice.

"Yeah, sure, but Torey, what the hell? Where were you all night, and why do you look like you've been crying? What the hell is going on?" Linds asked with real concern in her voice.

We were all walking side by side and it was pitch black out. *This is probably the easiest time I'll ever have to tell this story. And, I trust these girls.*

As we walked back to our dorm, I gave Linds and Sarah the lengthiest rendition of what had happened with Samantha, Greg, and me that I had ever told. It took me about 15 minutes. It was something to the effect of "Samantha was sleeping with our gymnastics coach, and then he got married and had a kid, and then he kissed me when I was fifteen, and then Samantha and I spent the night at his house, and then he moved away."

They had some questions that I answered, and I heard myself saying, "It wasn't that big of a deal for me. Samantha's situation was way worse than mine."

We ended up at their dorm room laying on pillows, with enough of a buzz that we kept talking. Linds shared a story of a high school boyfriend who was physically abusive in sadistic ways, and Sarah said she was raped by a boyfriend. Anger and hurt were swirling around inside me with the alcohol, and I couldn't decipher which was what.

At least my friends are as messed up as I am. Why do all three of us have a story like this, and we're only eighteen? My story isn't that big of a deal. Samantha, Linds, and Sarah ALL have stories WAY WORSE than mine.

*

Chapter Eleven:
Confrontation on Campus

Winter 1996

I laid on the plaid couch of our second-floor apartment, head pounding from too much tequila the night before, remote in hand, staring blankly at the TV yet not hearing it at all. Both my roommates were gone for the weekend, and wouldn't be back until that night. It was my junior year at Ohio State and I had a job coaching gymnastics while I also took more than twenty credit hours of pre-med classes and still managed to squeeze in partying.

Why did I drink so many shots of tequila? Why do I keep hanging out with him? Why does he keep hanging out with me? Why do we have so much fun together? God, I love him so much it hurts. I know he likes me, so why doesn't he just break up with her? God, this is just torture. This has gone on way too long. I'm done.

I had made the decision, it was time to be done with "Chemboy." Even if he was freaking gorgeous, it was time to get over his tall, dark mysteriousness and move on to something real. It was time to let go of those insanely blue eyes, huge hands, and quiet, dry sense of humor.

He's practically married, this is stupid. I'm going to call him and invite him over, and tell him that we can't be "friends" (or whatever it is that we are) anymore. I can't keep doing this. It's tearing me apart. I'm so in love with him, and I can't take anyone else seriously. I haven't dated anyone since we met. I'm pathetic. This is college, this is when I'm supposed to meet my husband. What am I doing?

I had been chasing him for two years now, since we met in Chemistry class (hence "Chemboy"). About nine months into us studying and partying together, yet NEVER touching each other, I found out from his roommate that he had a girlfriend.

What the hell? I thought we were going somewhere.

They'd been dating for five years, since he was fifteen, and she was at another college, so not around much. I remembered the feel of his body against mine the night before while we danced at the bar. There was an energy that was practically palpable between us. I wanted to kiss him SO BADLY. Chemistry? Yeah, we had it.

Why had he never told me about her? Why does he act like he likes me? Why does he smile at me like that? If we're just friends, he would have told me. He totally likes me. What do I have that she doesn't?

As I laid there on the couch, I thought about how amazing the night before had been. My friend Anna had met me at my apartment and then we met Chemboy, otherwise known as Brian, and his roommates at Ledo's. Wolfgang Parker and the Jumping Terrors, a ska/punk band that got everyone on the dance floor, was playing. There was tequila. There was dancing. There was a lot of me and Chris right up next to each other, but still NOT together. We had never kissed or even held hands, but dancing was fair game, and we danced a lot. My whole body hurt thinking about how much I want to be with him. I flopped onto my stomach, realizing I couldn't stop my pinball brain.

What the hell am I doing with him? He's never going to break up with her. I can't date anyone else because I am SO IN LOVE WITH HIM. Screw it, I'm done. I'm going to call him. This has to be over.

I dragged my hungover ass up off the couch, and walked to the phone on the wall. I picked up the receiver, took a big deep breath, and dialed his number. Ring, ring, ring.

"Hello?" one of his roommates answered.

"Hi, is Brian there?" I asked quietly, my head pounding like my skull was a maraca.

"Yeah, hold on a second," I heard a faint "B, phone's for you" in the background, and I waited. My heart was racing. My palms were sweating.

Can I really do this? Can I "break up" with a guy I am not even dating? Maybe more importantly, do I want to? I mean, what if he finally did break up with her? Then what? I shook my head, *I can't think that way, this situation is killing me.*

"Hello?" I heard his deep voice on the other line, and pictured his tall strong body standing at the phone, leaning against the wall, his longish dark brown hair hanging over one eye. I could see his blue eyes and mischievous look through the phone.

Hottest. Guy. Ever. Ugh. This is SO painful.

"Hi, it's Torey." I was shaking and there was a pit in my stomach, but I knew that I had to do this.

"Hey, how are you feeling today?" he asked, and I could hear the smirk. His 210 pounds could outdrink me any night.

"Rough, but that's not why I'm calling. We need to talk. We need to talk while sober. Can you come over tonight at 6?" I asked while my hands shook.

"Yeah, I can do that. Is everything okay?" he asked with a hint of concern.

"No, but I need to tell you face to face. Can you just come over later?" I hoped he couldn't hear the slight shake in my voice.

"Yeah, I'll be there. See you then," he said quietly before hanging up the phone.

See, he must like me to just agree to come with no more prodding or concern. He wants to hang out with me. Well, at least he loves me and respects me enough to come see me.

I couldn't help but think of a weird parallel between this relationshit, and the crazy ass one with Greg. Brian and I had everything I wanted in so many ways, but it wasn't allowed. It wasn't real, because he was with his girlfriend and I was "just a friend."

I love him even more because he HASN'T cheated on her.

What the hell? Why is this love shit SO HARD? I still haven't had a good relationship since Matt in high school, and that ended badly. I felt betrayed and tossed aside. Now, I am spending all my college years chasing this man who is practically married. I do love him, but I can't keep torturing myself spending time with someone that I want on a totally different level than what he can give. I'm done.

My mind flickered back to the studying I should be doing.

Yuck, I hate my organic chemistry classes. Brian is the only good thing about chemistry at Ohio State, and is he even good? I wish all my classes were like my English classes, where I could lose myself in books and writing. It's so amazing that I can get A's in English honors classes when I can barely eek by with C's in the O-chem classes. Maybe I shouldn't go to chiropractic college. Maybe the only reason I want to go to chiropractic college is because of Greg. Maybe I shouldn't base my life's purpose on advice from a guy who cheated on his wife with my friend and I? Ugh. I could lay on this couch all day and feel shittier and shittier.

I pushed the power button on the remote and got up and went to my room. I hated being hungover, but it seemed the rare Saturday or Sunday morning that I wasn't. Every morning that I felt bad, I swore I wouldn't drink the next night, and then the next night, when someone offered me a beer, I said yes.

I have no willpower. I'm totally out of control with alcohol. How can everyone else do this every weekend and still have their shit together? I totally suck. I'm not even a good sister or friend because I will ditch anyone and everyone for a chance to spend more time with Brian. I just suck. No wonder he doesn't want to be with me, I'm not good enough for him.

My bed was in the corner of my room and my green comforter was neatly on top. There were two windows in my room and lots of natural light on a good day. My desk was under one of them, but I couldn't bring myself to read. I laid down on my bed with my face in the covers. My fluffy orange and white cat, Body (named after Patrick Swayze's character in Point Break), jumped up on the bed next to me and I petted his head.

I should be studying. What the hell am I going to say to him tonight? "Hi, Brian, I'm in love with you, and it's the most joyful torture to be around you, but I just can't do it anymore?" *No way. I can't say that. I should go for a run. I'll clear my head, and get a workout at the same time.*

I begrudgingly got up off the bed and put my running clothes on. It looked pretty cold and windy out, so I grabbed a windbreaker to wear over my shirt. I was glad I didn't have to coach that day. The Level four and five gymnast's competitive season was almost over, and this was a rare weekend when they didn't have a meet.

God, I love those girls, I thought as I grabbed my key and headed for the door. I trotted down the steps in my spandex pants and Sauconys as the chatter in my head continued.

What am I going to say to him? "Brian, I can't keep hanging out with you because it's killing me," or "Brian, I really love hanging out with you, but it's just not that good for me." *He knows. He already knows all of this, and he's known for a while. I'm sure his roommates have all told him I'm in love with him, even if he's too blind or naïve to see it. If he wanted to have his cake and eat it too, why didn't he ever try anything? At least he's never cheated on her. At least he loves me and respects me enough not to just use me for sex, because it would have been hard to turn him away. He's a good guy.*

I started jogging down Lane Avenue toward High Street, finding my pace and hoping the headache would ease up as I got a few miles in. As I ran, my pinball thoughts bounced back to my life and what the hell I was going to do with it.

What do I do if not chiropractic college? I don't want to be a doctor. I don't want to be a nurse. I did pre-med and now I'm stuck. I like my biology classes, but chemistry, calculus, and biochemistry have all been miserable. I love my English classes, but English majors never get real jobs, right? Writers never make any money. I'd love to be a travel journalist, but that's not going to happen. I have to do something with this pre-med honors biology degree and the most obvious thing is medicine; it's already too late to change.

I was passing Mean Mr. Mustard's, a local bar and dance club, when I heard someone call out my name. "Votaw!" It was Brad, my old friend from our freshman dorm. He lived on South Campus now, and we still had classes together, but it seemed like it had been a long time since we lived in the dorms together. Two years is an eternity in college life.

Two years of chasing Chemboy.

"Hey, Brad" I said and gave him a quick hug. "I'm doing the 5th Avenue loop. I'll see you in micro this week."

"Okay, faster, Votaw, faster!" he yelled at me as I jogged away.

Running. I never thought I'd be a runner. I am a gymnast. I am a diver. I am not a runner.

I was slow, but I could sort of lose myself in it now. I never wore headphones, I just ran. I could think more clearly when my body was moving.

Okay, really, what am I going to say to him? I would have to drop classes in order to not see him next quarter, but I need some space and it has to be clean. It's worth it. I can't be in class with him every week and make the break. I'll let him continue in the series that we're in, and I'll take a quarter off O-Chem. I might be able to be done with it anyway depending on whether or not Biochem can fill the same requirement for graduation. I'll check with my advisor and figure out a way to do it and still graduate next year. I only have one quarter left this year. This might lead to taking a class or two over summer quarter, but it's worth it. I have to stop this obsession.

I rounded the turn from High Street to 5th Avenue and upped my pace a little.

Nothing like a five-mile jog to kick a hangover.

It was windy and starting to rain, or maybe snow a bit; sometimes in Ohio it's hard to tell the difference. I shivered, and my thoughts went back to the evening ahead.

I need to clean up the apartment and vacuum before he comes over tonight. If I'm going to break up with a guy I'm not

126

*even dating, the place should look presentable, right? This is
beyond ridiculous. My roommates will both be gone until late, so
we'll have the place to ourselves. What the hell am I doing, really?
What's wrong with me? Why does he hang out with me so much,
and invite me to do stuff with him if he's dating someone else? I
get that she's not at OSU, but it seems wrong to lead me on like
this when he knows I am smitten. He is ALL I think about when it
comes to guys. Greg and I still write now and then, but he's just a
friend and mentor. He might ask detailed questions about my love
life, but all in all, I'd say that relationship is completely platonic
now. I don't think about him in that way, and I never really did,
that stuff just happened, and I really wish it hadn't. I only reach
out to him if I need life advice, and usually only school or family
advice, not guy advice. Maybe I should talk to him about
chiropractic college, but I know he'll just push me to do it, and I'm
not sure that's right anymore.*

    I looked at my watch: eight minutes and thirty seconds per
mile. I was hungover, but I was still running at a decent pace for
my non-runner body. I rounded the last turn back onto Lane
Avenue, and knew I only had a mile left. The headache was mostly
gone. It felt good to have the rain on me and I surprised myself by
choking up a bit thinking about telling Chemboy goodbye. If there
were tears, they were mixed with rain, but I hadn't cried in so long
that even the hint of tears shook me. As much as sad, it just made
me angry.

    *Why do I fall in love with a guy who already has a
girlfriend? It's like I am destined to be miserable.*

    Only a mile to go, I cranked up the pace and pushed my
body hard enough to shut off my brain, if even for just a few
minutes.

    I am my own worst nightmare, I thought as I kicked hard up
the last few blocks and back to our apartment.

    I walked in and glanced at the clock. One hour 'til "go
time." I stripped off the cold wet running clothes, and jumped in a
near skin-scalding shower.

    I can do this. This is what needs to happen.

I put on my favorite jeans and my Lollapalooza t-shirt that reminded me of Brian because he had commented on it when we first met. I remembered his smile when I'd told him I'd seen Pearl Jam and the Red Hot Chili Peppers.

I didn't do makeup.

This is not worthy of makeup.

I vacuumed and cleaned up the kitchen.

I'm going to do this in the living room. He can't come in my bedroom, I thought as I straightened the chairs and folded the blanket on the couch.

5:55 p.m. I went to the bathroom and brushed my teeth again.

Why do hangovers make me feel like I want to eat all day, but I never feel better or full?

My stomach hurt, but I was sure that this was the right thing. I knew this was the only way for me to get over him and potentially move on. He'll be here any minute. I fidgeted and went to my room to put on some music.

What do you play at a funeral? Creedence Clearwater Revival, I thought. "Born on the Bayou" started slowly emanating from my room as I walked the few feet out to the living room.

I am pacing. Calm down, Torey.

I heard the downstairs door open and his huge frame coming up the stairs.

God, I love how tall he is. I love how smart he is. I love the way he dresses. I love that he has a mountain bike. I love that he could easily pick me up. Shit, this is going to suck.

When I heard the knock at the door, I opened it and there he stood. Long dark brown hair pulled back into a short ponytail, crystal blue eyes that could pierce my brain and regularly did. I looked up at all 6' 5" of him practically ducking to get in the door.

"Hi," I said, feeling even smaller than the 5'2'' I am.

"Hey. It's ugly out there," he said as he shook off his coat.

"Yeah, I went running a while ago. It is ugly. Can I take your coat?" I asked hesitantly.

This is going to be awful.

"Sure." He mirrored my hesitation just a bit. As he handed it to me, I noticed that when holding the hood at my eye level it almost touched the ground.

He's so freaking tall.

I hung his coat on the chair at my desk and went back out to the living room.

"What's going on?" He looked straight at me, his eyes full of concern.

"Ugh, a lot, and nothing all at the same time."

"Hmmm. That doesn't sound good." He leaned against the back of the couch and came down closer to my height.

"Let's sit down. Do you want something to drink?"

"No thanks, I'm okay." He smiled shyly and walked over to sit down on the far end of the couch.

I followed him and sat on the other side, leaving a few feet between us.

"So, I don't really know how to say or do this, so I'm just going to start talking." I said, pissed that I could hear my voice waver.

"Okay, I'm listening." He was obviously a little worried.

"I think you know that if I had it my way, we'd be more than just friends, right?" I didn't even give him time to answer, I just kept talking. "You're the only guy that I have any feelings for and the amount of time we spend together in and outside of classes is starting to kill me. I have to take some time away from you. I can't imagine dating anyone because you are the only person I think about, even though I know you have a girlfriend. I have so much fun with you, and I love spending time with you, but I want more than what you can give me, and this is just not fair anymore."

Holy shit, I just said that. Good work, Torey.

There was a long pause, but then he looked at me and said, "I get it. I really like hanging out with you too; but if this is what you need, I'll do what I can to help." He looked right at me with those freaking blue eyes and I was so glad he didn't discount what I had said.

Keep going, Torey, and make sure he knows the extent of the plan.

"I'm going to drop the next O-Chem class and pick up something else to fill that slot. I'm not going to take any classes with you next quarter and, as much as it kills me, I will avoid all parties that you might be at. I'm not going to call you or seek you out in any way. I really need a serious break from hanging out, so that maybe by the time I see you again I can really think of you as just a friend."

My stomach hurts and I am shaking, but holy shit. I am kicking ass at this. Maybe I should have done this a long time ago.

His eyes widened at the extent of my plan. "Really? You are going to drop classes? You don't really have to do that, Torey."

I like hearing him say my name.

"Yes, I do. I know I won't be able to do this if I have to see you three times a week. I need some space. It's not that big of a deal for me to drop that class. I have all next year, and summer if I need it, to still graduate in four years. I can do it."

"Not too many people graduate in four years," he said smiling at my life plan.

"I will. I'm not lazy and I'm not staying in Ohio any longer than I have to."

Seriously, I need to get out of this place.

"Well that doesn't surprise me. You're always talking about getting out of this place." He smiled again. He knew me well.

"Yep. Grey days and mediocrity are not my thing. I'll live at the beach or the mountains eventually, and you'll marry Doreen and have five kids," I said with a sarcastic smirk.

"I don't know about that. As much as you think you know me, maybe you don't know it all. There's more than just five years together that makes her important to me. I just can't give that up, even though I do have feelings for you."

What? What did he just say? Seriously? My stomach flipped over and my heart rate sped up. *Did he really just say that he had feelings for me?*

"What do you mean you have feelings for me?" I said, trying hard to be nonchalant.

"I know you know," he said. "What am I supposed to do? I can't break up with her. We've been together too long, and it's just not that easy."

"You're supposed to tell me that you have a girlfriend when you first meet me, not let me find out from your roommate nine months later," I said as I felt my heart racing and my palms starting to sweat.

This is not the conversation I was expecting. Did he just say he has feelings for me? Thank God, I am not a complete lunatic imagining all this!

"I know, I should have told you. I don't know why I didn't. I'm sorry." His tone was sincere, and it just made me like him even more.

This is torture. Ugh, in so many ways he is such a good guy, but I can't keep being friends with a guy I'm in love with.

"Well it is what it is now. I just need some time away from you to let the whole possibility of you get out of my head," I said shakily as the reality of what I was doing began to settle in. I would not be seeing him at parties, studying with him, rollerblading down the parking garage at 3 a.m. with him.

This relationshit is over.

"Okay, I understand. I guess I should probably go?" he asked with a questioning and somewhat resigned look.

"Yeah, I don't know what else there is to say. I'll reach out if and when I think it's safe for me to hang out with you again."

"You make it sound like I'm an axe-murderer," he laughed and I could see the twinkle in his blue eyes.

"Maybe worse," I smiled back as he stood up. As hard as this was, I knew it was the best thing. I had to stop this, and there was no way for me to stop these feelings when I was with him so much. There was that stupid pit in my stomach again, but I stood up with him and went to my room to get his coat.

I took a deep breath and handed him his coat. He reached out to take it and our hands touched, and I watched with sadness as he put it on.

"Can I give you a hug?" he asked with a genuine smile

"I suppose," I said with same smartass tone I used when I first told Greg I loved him. I didn't mean for it to come out like that. I really wanted a hug from him, but I was just mad that I was right all along.

He DOES like me. I'm just not worth breaking up with Doreen.

He wrapped his huge arms around me. The height difference made the possibility of a kiss non-existent, but the hug felt amazing and maybe like the first real thing that had happened between us. The truth was out. I had told him how I felt and it felt good to know that he knew. I hugged his chest like a ten-year-old hugging her dad. It felt so good to be close to him when sober and after that huge conversation; it felt like everything was somewhat okay. We both knew where we stood and I wouldn't continue to be his fill-in OSU pseudo-girlfriend. After a long minute, we both pulled away.

We were right at the door, and he said a quick goodbye and disappeared into the rainy night.

Holy shit. I just did that. I "broke up" with Chemboy. I took control of some aspect of my happiness. It sucks now, but I do feel a little sense of relief. Maybe I'm going to be okay?

I went to my room and changed into sweats. I numbly walked to the bathroom and brushed my teeth. I turned off Creedence, and put on George Winston, *Winter*.

I love this quiet piano.

I laid down in my bed in the dark and listened to the rain hit the roof. I felt empty, like a shell with nothing inside.

I have been pouring all this emotion and all this energy into him, and the possibility of us for close to two years…what now? I just shut that faucet off and in some ways, I feel a little fuller. Maybe everything will be okay. Maybe I'll find someone who wants what I want.

There were no tears, but I was exhausted physically from tequila and running, and emotionally from everything else. Next thing I knew, it was morning and the sun was shining on a fresh inch of snow.

Chapter Twelve:
Musing in the Mountains

Winter 2001

I skied forward as the chair in front of me scooped up the snowboarders ahead of us. My friend Betty and I were skiing off Chair 6, and it was a beautiful blue bird day in Breckenridge, Colorado. She sat down next to me on the chair and we relaxed a little before more leg-burning telemark turns.

Betty was my closest friend, and she looked similar enough to me that people often mistook us for one another. At some point, we just gave up correcting them. We worked together as medical assistants at Mountain Medical Center in town, which meant, unfortunately, that we usually only got to ski on the weekends. The good thing about Chair 6 is that it is up higher on the mountain, and the terrain is mostly black diamonds, so it keeps the gapers (tourists) away.

We're locals. We know this whole mountain.

It was a Saturday, and we were two twenty-four-year-old girls enjoying no lines and sunny skies on the massive mountains of Breckenridge, Colorado.

Life is good.

This was my third year of what was supposed to be one year off between undergrad and chiropractic college. One year wasn't long enough in the mountains, but it was long enough to decide against chiropractic college. While the mountains were magnetic and energizing, I had a creeping feeling that I was wasting my (career) life away too.

I can't keep making $12 an hour forever and working three jobs, even if it is in an incredible place.

As we sat there taking in the beauty, Betty asked, "When's Brian coming back?"

Just the mention of his name brought a flutter to my heart, and I smiled. "He should be back in the next week. He is just helping his mom finalize all the financial stuff, and then he's coming back," I said with a huge smile in anticipation of his return.

"What a good guy to go back to Ohio and help take care of his dying father. Not every guy our age would do that. He's the real deal, Torey," Betty chirped with an air of jealousy.

"I know. He is a good guy. It hasn't been easy for him, but I do think it's been good for him. Did you know that I chased after Brian for two years in college, while he had a girlfriend and finally had to 'break up' with him even though we weren't even dating?" I laughed thinking back to that painful conversation.

"Ha! That's hilarious. How'd you finally get together?" Betty's eyebrows danced with curiosity.

"A year after I 'broke it off,' we had classes together again. I had been dating a great guy, so I thought all was well and I could handle seeing Brian. But one day, he and I were biking back from class together, and he told me that he and his girlfriend had broken up. I about shit myself. He said something like 'the ball being in my court,' so I went home, freaked out a bit, then broke up with my boyfriend the next day. I wouldn't have been able to be in that relationship anymore anyway, knowing I had a chance with Brian. There was just way too much chemistry between us. We got together a few days later." I shook my head at what a crazy love story we had.

"Ah, true love!" Betty exclaimed with a smile. "I can't imagine."

I wish... I do feel like Brian and I are meant to be together, but it's so up in the air right now. He's so far away. I wish I never

would have broken up with him last year. I'm such a bitch. "Full-
on bitch," *one of my friends would say.*

"Well, maybe, but maybe not since I ditched him for some
random guy after not even a year in Colorado. Brian and I broke
up because I wasn't happy he didn't have any thoughts on what we
should do with our future, and during that time his dad was
diagnosed with cancer. Thank God he reached out to me as a friend
and then we stayed in touch when he went back to Ohio. I really
thought Brian and I had it all, but I couldn't stand it that, when I
decided not to go to chiropractic college, he didn't have any
opinion on what we should do. His response was basically, 'I'll do
whatever you want,' which made me feel like he didn't care at all
and our life plan was my responsibility. What's with guys our age
and their indifference to what they want?" I didn't try to hide my
snide tone. The question was mostly rhetorical, but I thought to
myself, *Can any guy ever live up to what I think I want?*

"I don't know, but I've never been happy with a guy my
age. That's why I love John. He's a man." Betty's face had a
dreamy sort of look that kind of creeped me out.

"Yeah, but I really want someone close to my age, someone
I can plan my life with. I can't wait for Brian to come back so we
can figure out what's next for us. He keeps saying he can't wait to
see me, and it seems like we'll get back together when he gets
back. We'll see." My heart raced as I thought about seeing him
again. Next to Matt from high school, Brian was the second guy in
my life I felt like I was really in love with.

I wonder if we can make it work.

We were coming to the top of the chair and, as we popped
off, I asked, "Amen?" referring to the run we might take.

"Sure," Betty cheered, as she and I skated to the left toward
one of our favorite runs. I'd been telemarking for two years and
Betty had been tele-ing for about as long. I loved the fluidity of my
heel being free and the all-encompassing movement that tele skiing
allowed. It was the only time I ever felt graceful. I paused at the
top of "Amen" and found my line. As I started down, I felt my
right leg take the weight as my left shot out in front and I turned to

the right. Lunge, lunge, lunge. Swoosh, swoosh, swoosh. It felt so good. My shoulders pointed downhill as my legs and hips twisted under me, dancing up and down, while I wiggled though the moguls and between the trees. I felt the wind on my face and was glad I had my helmet on to keep me warm and safe. There's nothing quite as freeing as flying down a hill, pulled by gravity, in control, but right on the edge, where one wrong move could shoot you headfirst into a tree.

I love this. Skiing is amazing. I love the blue skies and the wind and grandness of Colorado. How did I ever live in Ohio?

Betty was skiing to the left of me. Our techniques were different, but we could both ski any slope you dropped us on. When we skied together, we got some attention from the chair now and then. "Nice turns, Ladies!" with a whistle or two wasn't uncommon. We were hot commodities, at least on the surface. We were cute, smart, athletic girls with money-making potential.

Who wouldn't want to date us?

As I was dancing down the mountain, my mind flashed back to all the times I had with Brian since we got together, and since graduating from Ohio State. He and I both worked on fishing boats in Alaska to save money to move to Colorado. When we got to Colorado, we lived together and shared a car. I was only 22, but I was sure I wanted to be with him forever. I was in for the long haul, until it seemed like he was just along for the ride.

He's so smart and has the potential to do anything. Why does it seem like I'm the only one looking to the future? I hope when he comes back to Colorado, he's clearer about what he wants. It's been hard not to feel close to him. His reaching out to me emotionally while his dad was dying has brought us closer again, even though we haven't dated in almost a year.

Woop! I missed a turn and went straight over a mogul, almost losing control, which snapped me back to the moment at hand. I recovered and didn't fall, but that move was less than graceful.

I'm glad we're not under the lift.

Betty was up ahead of me and I saw her turn down left onto

"Boneyard" and head back to Chair 6. I caught up and slid into the lift gate right next to her. Betty and I were adept at conversing in chunks while skiing together and our conversation picked up where it had left off.

"So, when's the last time you saw John, anyway?" I asked.

"Last week, but we are going to Florida together in a couple months." Betty smiled as she said it, and I marveled at the confidence she had when talking about him.

"Really, how does he explain that to his girlfriend?" I tried to hide my feelings about the situation.

"I don't know. I don't ask about that. It's never really been a problem because he does so much stuff separate from her. He has a lot of friends that he hangs out with too, so I don't think she really keeps tabs on him." Betty seemed to have no reservations about this relationship and showed no guilt or shame.

How does she do that?

John was about twenty years older than Betty and they had been "together" ever since she was in college, so that was close to seven years. He lived with a woman but wasn't married to her, and his relationship with Betty was not public, but Betty thought of it as completely okay. When she first told me, I couldn't help but think about Greg and Samantha. I told Betty about what had happened with me, Greg, and Samantha, but I don't think she saw the parallel. There was, however, an unspoken understanding that we were both messed up enough to "get" each other. I remember thinking when we first met, *Wow, she's as f-ed up as I am. I think we can be friends.*

"Do you think your thing with John affects being able to find someone to date?" I tried to sound purely curious.

"I don't know. I've been with John for so long and through two live-in boyfriends. He's just John. He's always been there for me since my brother died, and I know I can count on him." Her tone was matter-of-fact.

"But, do you think it's good for you?" I asked, trying to sound innocent and like I didn't have a strong opinion about what her answer should be.

"Good shmood, who knows?" She laughed and quickly changed the subject. "What are you doing tomorrow?"

"Going climbing on the Front Range, I think, or maybe Buena Vista. It's a good weekend when I get to ski *and* climb!" I said and then added, "But, what about tonight? Are we going to Eric's ?"

Downstairs at Eric's was the local pizza joint/bar that we frequented. As I was talking to her, I glanced toward the t-bar going up to Peak 8.

I wonder how the snow is up there.

There were a few people hiking clear to the top, and it was a perfect day for it. We could see Mount Baldy behind us and Quandary Peak to the south.

"Yeah, I think that's the plan. Pizza and beer—always good." Betty crinkled her nose at how simple it was to have fun.

We were reaching the top again, and I noticed that my legs were starting to feel a little jello-y. We'd been skiing for several hours already, and black diamond tele turns weren't something I could do all day without being shot.

"Solitude?" I suggested, referring to another run off Chair 6.

"Sure, and then let's head over to the t-bar." She nodded her head toward it.

Sweet! That's where I want to be.

"Yes! I like it. Are you up for hiking Peak Seven?" I hoped she'd do the hike with me because I was craving the space up there, but I didn't want to do it alone.

"Nah, not today. I want to get home, clean my place, and get groceries before going out. Hey, what's up with PA school? Have you finished applying?" Betty's gaze caught mine, and I could see her concern.

"Yeah, I applied to four schools, but I doubt I'll get in because I don't have the required hours in the medical field yet. I'll be close by the spring, so I'm hoping they'll take that into consideration, but we'll see. If I don't get in, I'll hang here, ski and climb one more year, and get more hours at Mountain Medical. It'd be awesome to get in this year, and get grad school over with, but I'm not holding my breath," I felt a bit of anxiety growing inside my chest just thinking about the possibility of that huge commitment.

"I bet you'll get in. It'll be my luck that you and Hil both get in, and I'll be left here with no friends again," she sulked.

"Aw," I smiled and bumped her shoulder with mine, "Are you going to miss me?"

"Yeah, whose hockey games am I going to watch? And, who's going to introduce me to men my age?"

I laughed at her ornery smile. "Good point. I probably should stay to help you out with your love life."

We skied for another hour or so, taking runs off the t-bar, and then headed back to the bus at Peak Eight, which would drop us off at our cars in town. My body was tired, and it felt good.

I love feeling like my body is just done and it's only two in the afternoon. I have earned my beer tonight.

We went to our respective homes, and while Betty responsibly cleaned and bought groceries, I curled up in my bed with a good book. Skiing is the one sport that makes me crave a nap, and it wasn't long before I was deep in slumber.

The phone woke me and I glanced down to see who it was—Brian, nice!

"Hey!" I bubbled, unable to contain my excitement.

"Well, hello there, Little One!" he replied warmly.

"I'm not that little. You are just a giant," I sassed. "I got in tons of runs on Chair 6 this morning with Betty, it was beautiful out. I can't wait 'til you are back here and we can ski together." I smiled at the thought of having him close again.

"Soon enough, soon enough. I am hoping to leave tomorrow. My friends are having a party for me tonight and so I just called to say hi before I go out."

"Sounds like fun. Be careful. Those boys in Ohio all drink too much." I'm sure he heard the worry in my voice.

"Yeah, and those girls in Breckenridge all drink too much too. You be careful yourself." I could see his smirk and twinkling blue eyes in my mind.

He's so hot.

"Will do. Brian, I can't wait to see you!"

I really, really can't wait to see him!

"Me too. Bye, Babe." He said it with a confident tone that I hadn't heard in his voice since his dad had been sick. He sounded good.

"Bye." I smiled and hugged my pillow as I hung up the phone.

God, I miss him. What's going to happen when he gets back? I wish I knew that we were going to be okay. If he asked me to marry him, I would say "yes" in a heartbeat. I know we have some things we need to work out, but I think my biggest stress is just the commitment part. He's totally back in my head, just like in college. I can't see my life without him in it. I'll give it a chance when he gets back, and see if he can step up and move forward with me. I love it here in Breckenridge so much, but I can't keep working for nothing, barely able to cover my bills, forever. This place is so touristy, I could never start a family here. I don't want my kids to grow up in the mountain equivalent of Disneyland. But I'm not going back to Ohio, ever. I need to get going and start my career. I need to put some money in a retirement account. I love skiing, climbing, and playing hockey and I feel so confident in all those things now—I just can't keep up this party lifestyle forever. I want more. I want to feel proud of what I do for work, not just proud of what I do for fun. I want a husband and kids. I want a house and a dog. I want stability.

Chapter Thirteen:
Climbing in Queen Creek

Spring 2002

"What?" I asked totally dumbfounded.

"Torey, they just called your name. Go already!" my friend Susan cheered as she pushed me toward the stage. I handed my beer to her, and started toward the awards area. I was still just wearing a tank top and shorts, even though the sun had gone down and it was starting to get dark.

Brrr... The desert gets cold fast.

"Second place, locals, age 20-25, Torey Votaw," the announcement rang out again, just as I reached the stage. Someone shook my hand, handed me a voucher ticket to take to the awards tent, and pointed me toward it.

What the heck? I'm not a good enough climber to be placing at a bouldering contest! There are professional famous climbers here. Is this for real?

I'd had one beer, and I was feeling a little buzzed after a long day climbing in the sun. Since starting Physician Assistant school eight months prior, I hardly ever drank, and my tolerance was LOW.

Beer plus surprise win makes Torey a happy girl, I thought as I walked up to the awards tent.

My friends from PA school, Susan and Stephanie, met me on my way to pick up my winnings. Susan with her long dark hair,

141

rock hard body, and 'not fair' big boobs was wearing moonstone stickers on her nipples. And Steph, with her Jodie Foster face and rebellious Mennonite past, had a bumper sticker on her ass. The music was loud, the energy was high, and this party was happening! There's nothing like being outside in the desert at night with a bunch of happy climbers and beer.

I love these girls. For being smart as hell, they are totally cool and fun! Thank goodness they agreed to come with me, so I have some wing women.

"What'd you win?!" Steph asked, hopping up and down a little, with a sparkle in her piercingly blue eyes.

"I don't know yet. Let's go find out!" I held my arms out for them to link up and we started skipping. It felt so good to be outside, in the dark, with friends and other climbers, loud music, and boundless energy. Lately, far too many hours had been spent on a chair in lectures, or the law library at Arizona State University. This night was a much-needed flashback to my carefree play days in Breckenridge.

Yee haw!

I got to the awards tent and gave the attendant my voucher.

I thought, *Maybe I'll win a T-shirt or a chalk bag*, but she came back with a garbage bag full of stuff! *WHAT? This is all for me? Awesome!*

"Wow, thanks!" I looked at Susan and Stephanie with huge eyes, thinking, *I must be getting away with something, I'm not that good of a climber.*

"Let's go check this stuff out," I exclaimed, and we made our way back to the other climbers from my climbing gym, who we were hanging out with.

"Good job, Torey!" one of the guys from the gym said and gave me a high five. That prompted several more high-fives and some claps on the back.

I smiled, *this feels good.* I was much more a student than a climber, and I hadn't really felt quite part of this gang yet.

Maybe I do belong with this crowd?

I sat down on a bouldering pad and started pulling stuff out of the bag—new 5.10 climbing shoes, a Moonstone fleece, a chalk bag, two t-shirts, a water bottle, a mug, drink tickets, and a bunch of bars and coupons. Susan and Steph were next to me, pulling things out and sticking more stickers in inappropriate places.

Hehe. I smiled. *WOW! This is amazing.*

"Holy crap, there's like $300 worth of stuff in here! I guess the $25 entrance fee was worth it. I can't believe I placed!" I was in serious awe of this new development.

"Well, you do go to the climbing gym all the time, and you're like a freaking spider!" Susan said laughing.

I smiled at her and Stephanie, then handed them the drink tickets. "Let's go put this stuff away and take advantage of the free drinks!"

Just as we were getting up to walk away, another guy from my gym came back with a bag of his own.

"Hey, what'd you get?" I asked.

"First place, locals, 25-30," he said with a tip of his brown-haired head and a shy smile. He was tall and thin, but didn't have the rock-hard body of a typical hardcore climber. There was something soft and sweet about him.

"Cool, congrats, good for you! There's a ton of good swag in there. Let's have a celebratory drink together when I get back?." I held out my hand.

"Sounds good," he said, smiling innocently as he shook my hand.

This guy looks way too 'boy next door' to be an awesome climber. I've definitely seen him in the gym, but I don't think we've ever talked.

I smiled back at him, grabbed my bag, and then linked arms with Susan who was already linked to Stephanie. It felt good to be with these two amazingly smart, beautiful, and freaking cool girls.

I'm so lucky.

The desert sky was starting to come out in full force, and as we walked away from all the lights and fire, the stars became brighter and brighter. The music was pumping, and it was easier to hear each other the further away we walked.

I love the desert. It feels so clean and crisp at night, a lot like Colorado, and not at all like humid Ohio.

It felt like the stars were surrounding me, injecting me with their magic and energy from across the universe. Ever since I read Edward Abbey's *Desert Solitaire,* and spent a weekend biking in Moab with Brian, I had been in love with the desert.

I tripped over a rock on the trail, and my attention was back on the night at hand, "Ugh! I need to put on some real shoes and a jacket."

"Who's that guy you were talking to, Torey?" Steph asked.

"I've seen him in the gym before, but I don't know him at all. He must be a really good climber to place in the men's local division. I think there were A LOT more guys than girls competing. He doesn't even really look like a climber; he doesn't have that cocky 'I'm a badass' look that a lot of climbers walk around with. He seems nice."

"Ah, you like him!" Susan nudged me and shot me a sassy smile.

"I don't even know him, but I'm happy to have a drink with him and celebrate our collective wins together! Ah! I climbed next to Tommy Caldwell today! This is nuts. It's so good to be here with you girls, and not studying freaking medicine this weekend! Thanks so much for coming with me!" I felt happier and more on top of the world than I had in months.

PA school was hard. I liked what I was studying, but I was not meant to sit for forty hours a week. That schedule just didn't work for me. Even when I got a few miles of running in before 6:00 a.m., all that sitting just made me nuts.

"Yeah! It's good to be camping and away from all the super nerds at PA school. Thanks for inviting us! And, Susan scored a bunch of free swag for showing off those lovely tits of hers too," Steph giggled.

"WHAT??? Susan, you total slut!" I laughed.

"What? I don't care. If they can earn me a free backpack, I'll take off my shirt. I've got no money. I live on loans just like you two do," Susan said with her sassy matter-of-fact, I-don't-give-a-shit-what-other-people-think tone.

She's awesome. If I had tits like that, I might use them for free swag too.

"Fair point. Did you really get a free backpack? That's big money." I smirked at her audacity.

"I'm working on it. I think if I bring them a beer or two, it's mine," she said casually.

"Too funny. You've got some ovaries, my friend." I was always amazed by her confidence.

"Torey, what's up with Brian? Didn't he come back last week? I haven't even gotten to talk to you about it yet," Steph asked as we dropped my bag of winnings off at my Subaru. My heart sank at the mention of him and us.

Brian and I had gotten back together in Breckenridge in the spring, and he had moved from Colorado to Arizona with me. But he never got a "real" job and it seemed like his presence was more stressful than helpful. He decided to go back to work on the fishing boats in Alaska, and I didn't want that at all. The long distance and the very different life situations were the beginning of the second end for us.

"Yeah, that's done," I said, as I reached into the back of my car and grabbed a jacket. I sat down, and started taking off my sandals to switch them out for socks and shoes.

"What does that mean?" Susan wondered, though she didn't sound surprised.

"That means that I can't do long distance with him when I'm busting my ass in grad school. He's going from working in Alaska to raft guiding on the Gauley, and both those things are SO TOTALLY different than grad school. It's just too hard, when I am studying so much and working so hard, to see him just kind of coasting. And, don't even let me get into the raft guide thing. They'll all be living in their cars, smoking weed, and drinking too much. I'm not generally opposed to that, but I am for my 26-year-old boyfriend. I'd rather be planning a real life with him. UGH! I love that man to death, and I know he has a really good heart, but it just seems like we are in such different places that I can't make it work. I don't want to have to try so hard."

"Shit, that sucks, Tor, but I think you've known for a while. Just think, your raft guide boyfriend lasted six months longer than mine did while I was in PA school," Susan cajoled.

"That's still so crazy to me that we were both dating guys guiding in Buena Vista, when we got into PA school. What are the chances?" I shook my head.

"Well, they were both pretty freaking hot. I don't blame either one of you," Steph said with that dreamy look in her eye.

"Hey, I have Snapples in my car. Do you guys want to hang out here in the darkness and hydrate before we head back?" I was hoping for a little quiet with my friends.

"I don't know. There are a lot of hotties back there, but we've got all night...so I guess," agreed Steph.

"I'm down with whatever," Susan said as she stretched out my bouldering pad, laid back on it, and gazed up at the stars. "I can't hang with people who drink all night anyway—I'm a total lightweight."

"I hear you! I can't believe I have a buzz off just one and a half beers. I've been "Sober Sally" since starting PA school. I must admit, it feels good to let loose a little this weekend, and I can't think of anyone else I'd rather hang out with," I said as I laid down next to Susan. I handed them each a Snapple peach tea, and then opened my own.

"I can't believe you won! That's so awesome, Tor. I think you should go hook up with your counterpart winner to get your mind off Brian," Susan joked, but with a hint of seriousness.

"Hehe, thanks, that sounds like letting loose for sure. It's cool that they had a locals division; otherwise I wouldn't have won anything. I think I've been getting stronger since bouldering outside more this spring. I never thought I'd like bouldering, I always wanted to climb big traditional stuff. I'd love to take you guys climbing sometime. It's so good. It's like a puzzle for your body and your mind. There's nothing better to get your mind off all the bullshit of life. I don't worry about boys, jobs, parents or anything when I am climbing. I am completely fixated on the rock and what to do next. It's like your whole body has to be completely engaged to do it well. It feels good to be that focused, and for me it's not easy to get there."

"You mean, ah, you don't, ah, feel like that, ah, when Dr. P is lecturing, ah," Stephanie laughed as she said the last 'ah'.

"Ugh. If I never had to hear another lecture from him, it would be too soon. We have what, four more months 'til rotations?" I asked. Dr. P had a PhD, as well as the worst lecturing skills of any smart person ever. UGH, painful.

"Yeah, and there's a week off in August before we start rotations. We can make it." Susan sounded determined.

"Yes, we can. I'm done worrying about my grades though I rocked first quarter with a 3.8, but I just can't sit that much. I'm going climbing on the weekends and hanging on to a piece of my old self this last quarter. I care about school, but I was miserable not getting outside enough. I need a weekend at least once a month in the wide-open desert. Shooting star!" I pointed to it in the eastern sky above the rocks of Queen Creek.

"Nice, that's a sign. Let's get back to all those hotties and see which ones can handle us!" Stephanie said as she jumped up like a girl on a mission to get laid.

"Okay, okay. Let's go!" I rolled up and packed my bouldering pad into the back of my car.

It was dark enough by then, so we turned on our headlamps as we started down the boulder laden path, back to the raging party that was the PBC. We had stickers over most parts of us, and still just enough of a buzz (as partners in crime) to feel fearless and silly.

I saw the group of climbers from my gym, and that cute guy raised a beer at me and smiled as we came back to the group. He had on a puffy coat and seemed to always be smiling. He appeared to have a tight group of friends with him, and I eventually walked up next to him and restarted our conversation. Susan and Stephanie disappeared to the Marmot boys tent, not long after I started talking to him. It was cold, and he was happy to share his puffy coat with me, as long as he got to stay in it too.

This guy's pretty cute, and damn does it feel good to be held.

Even though I had technically had a boyfriend for the last three months, Brian had been gone and I'd been lonely both physically and emotionally.

Human touch. I miss this. I miss Brian, but that just isn't working right now. There's too much history to keep it light and fun. I want way more for us than what he can offer right now. I wonder if this is another 'to be continued' with us?

I felt lips on my neck and my mind snapped back to the night and the boy at hand. I looked up into his brown eyes and thought, *What the hell! I just want to have some fun. I'm tired of all the relationshit. Maybe I need a 'no big deal' kind of fling with this nonchalant climber boy.*

Chapter Fourteen:
Thriving in Three Rivers

Spring, 2004

I turned left into the small plaza holding the Thai restaurant where I was meeting a new girlfriend, and parked. The smell of orange blossoms had faded since I dropped into the valley, but it was still faint on the breeze. Brutus, my new black Lab/Aussie mix puppy, was sleeping in the back of the Subaru. He was tired enough from a little walk by the river on the way home from Three Rivers, that I knew he'd be fine sleeping in the back for an hour or so. I still had on my work clothes—a black pencil skirt with little red cherries and a tight sleeveless black top.

I'm pretty cute in this outfit, I thought as I grabbed my purse and got out of the car. I walked to the back and opened the hatch and looked at my new sweet puppy.

I love this little guy. He is so awesome.

I gave Brutus a snuggle and some water before closing the hatch on him for his naptime, and my dinner out.

I have a dog! I can no longer fit everything I own in my Subaru at one time. Does this make me a real adult? Have I "made it"?

I turned to walk toward the restaurant.

It'll be nice to have dinner with some new friends, I thought as I walked toward the door. *I wish it wasn't such a shit day though.*

149

Bells jingled as I opened the door, and I heard a little waterfall in front of me as I stepped into the restaurant. I glanced around and saw an open seat next to my new friend, and two guys with their backs to me on the other side of the table. She waved, and I smiled as I walked in and sat down next to her.

"Hey! How's it going?" I asked.

"Great, I'm glad you could make it. These are my friends..."

I didn't hear the first guy's name because I was immediately locked into the blue eyes on the guy seated across from me. I heard her again as she nodded to him, "...and Justin," she said. He smiled at me with those twinkly eyes and shook my hand rather formally. "Guys, this is Torey."

Holy shit, LOOK at that Justin guy's eyes. Those might be the bluest eyes I have ever seen.

"Hi, nice to meet you both," I said and then quickly glanced around to locate the server. "I need a beer."

"Ha! I like her already," Justin said with his bright white smile. He emanated HAPPY. He was thin and just a bit taller than me, from what I could tell while he was sitting down, but he just had this energy that seemed to surround him and pour into me. I felt a little flutter in my stomach.

The waitress must have heard me and hurried over. I ordered a Singha, which seemed to be what they were all drinking.

"What do you all do for work?" I asked, but I was really only interested in this Justin across from me.

"We're both biologists, and Justin works in the backcountry." My new friend said answering for all of them.

"And you work at the clinic in Three Rivers?" Justin asked as he leaned forward just slightly.

"Yes, I'm a physician assistant. We see patients just like doctors do. Dr. Rice is with me some days and some days I'm what you get." As I spoke the words, I felt the reality of the high level of responsibility I had at work and took a deep breath.

"Cool. Do you get to do stitches and stuff?" Justin probed.

"Yeah. Lots of fun stuff like that. But the best part of my job is Dr. Rice. He's just awesome. My patients are sweet and I love that Three Rivers is such a small town, yet there's a mix of a lot of different types of people. How do you like working in the backcountry?" I asked. Justin's blue eyes stared right into mine as he listened to me blabber on about my job, and our conversation didn't even pause.

It was already as if the other couple wasn't even there.

Why am I nervous? My heart is racing and I am talking fast. Calm down, Torey. Geez.

"I hike around and check on things, talk to people, sometimes help out of there's an emergency. I've heard of Dr. Rice, but I've never met him. He sounds like a crazy hippy doctor, which is perfect for Three Rivers."

Forget Dr. Rice and medicine! That might be the coolest job description I have ever heard.

"Dr. Rice is great. You'd love him, most people do. Your job sounds amazing. How cool!" I smiled when my Singha appeared. We toasted around the table and I took a long swig, trying to shift my energy from the hard day. "I'm sorry, I'm feeling kind of out of it. A good friend of mine's father died today, and I'm more shaken up about it than I thought I would be. I had just seen him and spent time at Christmas and he wasn't even sick then, but he went down fast. It's all kind of surreal, and it's been a rough day."

"Oh, Torey, I'm sorry, but I'm glad you are here with us and not home alone," my new girlfriend said.

Oh right, there are people sitting next to me and not just this crazy blue-eyed, strong-jawed, long-haired park ranger dude across from me. He. Is. Stunning.

"Yeah, thanks for the invite, I'm really glad to be here," I said, and my mind flashed back to another restaurant table a few months ago.

I was sitting with some of my PA friends at a restaurant in

Porterville. I was the only one of my friends who wasn't single and one of them asked me how I knew I was in love with my then boyfriend for a year and a half. Emotion overwhelmed me, and I broke down crying.

"I'm not," I had said through pathetic tears.

That night I went home that night and broke up with him. *I'm failing again and again.*

I'm an idiot. I suck with men. It seems like I am just constantly going from one guy to the next and I am ALWAYS the one breaking up with them. I'm such a bitch.

"Torey." Justin's voice brought me back to the Thai restaurant in Visalia. "I hear that you climb."

"Yes! I love it! It's what I do. I started in 1999 in Colorado and followed a lot of big trad (traditional) routes that first summer, but the last few years in grad school I did a lot more bouldering. I've only found a bunch of old guys to climb with so far here. Do you climb?" I asked, hoping I didn't sound as desperate as I felt. I longed for a climbing partner much more than a boyfriend but killing two birds with one stone would be great.

Those eyes are freaking amazing.

"I do climb," Justin said with a quirky formality.

Awesome.

"What kind of climbing do you like to do?" I coaxed.

No expectations, Torey, have no expectations. It's okay if he's a gymrat or only climbs 5.6.

"I'm all about trad. I love placing gear and doing big long routes," he replied enthusiastically.

YES!! This blue-eyed Justin is going to be my climbing partner! This is so good. Where's this guy from?

The waitress showed up to take our orders and Justin and I both ordered the Pad Thai with chicken. I didn't hear the other two order, I was so focused on this boy across from me it was as if I was in a tunnel connected to him.

I can feel this is the start of something good. Fresh start. I just bought a house. This is all good.

"Where are you from?" I asked, trying to keep the expectation out of my voice, as well as my head. I'd lived away from the Midwest long enough to realize that people from the Midwest were my people.

I love midwestern values and I want those in my partner.

"A small town in Wisconsin." He smiled big enough to reveal his amazing set of straight white teeth. "And you?"

Seriously, awesome!

"I'm from northeast Ohio." I was not able to contain my smile at our similar roots.

"Ah, a Buckeye?" He raised an eyebrow.

"Yes, to the point that my new puppy is named Brutus for Brutus Buckeye." I smiled at the thought of my new baby.

"You have a puppy?" Both eyebrows shot up with surprise."

"Yeah, he's in the car. He's the best. I have a house too. I just bought a house. I have a house, a dog, and a real job. It's like I'm an adult or something. Crazy!"

It was as if I was watching this successful woman from the outside.

Who am I? What happened to the messed-up girl drinking too much and making $12 an hour in Breckenridge?

"How old are you? And, where's your house?" he asked, obviously interested in knowing more about me.

"I'm 27, and the house is in Exeter. I like the small downtown part of Exeter; it reminds me of Ohio. And, I have big trees at my house. I committed to stay at my job for at least two years, so I figured I'd buy a house. I'll either rent it or sell it if I decide to move. And how old are you, Justin?" I asked, wanting to know more myself.

"I'm 25." Justin tipped his head and squinted a little as if he wondered if it mattered.

"How long have you worked in the backcountry?" I was both impressed and a bit jealous of a job like that.

"Three years now. I love being out there, so far from

everything. I really like my alone time, so it suits me well." He said it with passion and confidence.

"So, your grad school loans are paid off? That's nice!" He said shifting the focus back to me.

Are we being rude? I'm not sure I care.

I glanced at my girlfriend and she gave me a quick wink.

Ha! I think we're ok.

"A lot of my loans are paid off, but not all. PA school was expensive. I've never been in debt before and I don't like it. Now the house...ugh. I have First World debt now."

I don't want to talk about debt! Let's talk about climbing and living in the back country.

Our food came, and the conversation moved to summer music festivals and the incredible mountains that Justin got to call his office. He spoke of climbing dreams in the Sierra, and I could feel my heart melting as he described some of the routes on his tick list—fun names like Castle Rock Spire, Fishhook Arete, Bear Creek Spire, Mithral Diheral, and Moon Goddess Arete. He was a strong climber based on the routes he was talking about.

It would be so fun to run around in the mountains with this guy. Maybe this is it? Maybe my life is coming together? I mean, I do have a good job, and a house, and a sweet doggie. Maybe I've finally gotten my shit together enough to have a good relationship and not mess it all up? I don't know where this is going, but I'm sure I'm going to see this Justin from Wisconsin again.

Chapter Fifteen:
Confessions on a Couch

Spring 2006

As I drove to my therapist's office for the third appointment, tears streamed down my cheeks. I missed Justin so much, my body physically hurt. We'd spent the last year and a half together, climbing, playing, and planning a life, but it just wasn't right. We'd gotten engaged last July, but pretty quickly, I felt like something was missing. I couldn't name it, I just wasn't ready to plan a wedding; and that's not like me. I like to plan. When he said he wasn't sure he wanted kids, I knew I had to be done.

That's a deal-breaker. I want to be a mom.

In January, I cut out all alcohol to be as clear-headed and intentional as I could be with him. I wasn't going to give up on this easy. I was up front with what I wanted and what I needed, but Justin just kept pulling away. So, I gave the ring back and I had been a total mess for the past thirty days.

What is wrong with me?

I glanced at the letters sitting next to me in the passenger's seat.

Damned letters. I wonder why I have carried these things around for 15 years? It was not that big of a deal.

There were rust stains on the envelopes from when I used to keep them under my mattress at home.

Twelve years ago before I left for college. It's been so long, this can't be the issue.

I only brought three of the fifteen or so I had—the three with the most "incriminating evidence," as he wrote in one of them.

What am I even going to say to him about these? Where do I start?

I had been seeing my therapist, Gary, for a few weeks already, and I did really like him, but I didn't know if we were getting anywhere.

All I do is blubber on and on about breaking off my engagement with Justin. I'm such a mess. It's amazing that I go to work every day, and tell people how to feel better, when I feel like total shit.

I turned into the driveway and pulled into a parking spot.

I have to pee, I thought. *Maybe I can just give him the letters and then go to the bathroom? That'll give him a few minutes to read them without me sitting there awkwardly watching him. Ugh. I haven't talked about this stuff in SO LONG.*

I signed in at the window and sat down in a chair in the quiet brown reception area and waited. It was always quiet in there, especially considering the many therapist's offices it held. The letters sat next to me. I kept them at arm's length, instead of in my lap. They felt dirty to me. Just looking at them made my heart race and my palms sweat. I really liked Gary, and wasn't sure what he would think of the story that came with those letters.

Was it a big deal? My story was nothing compared to Samantha's. I flipped through a People magazine. *Brad Pitt, Angelina Jolie, Jennifer Aniston—seriously, who reads this shit? I guess it's nice to know famous movie stars have the same relationshit that I do. I wonder how Samantha's doing—if this shit with Greg is still impacting her, or if she's totally fine and normal.*

"Torey?" Gary called my name quietly as he poked his head around the door.

"Hi." I smiled back, and stood up to follow him to his office, letters in hand.

I really like this guy. He's got a very calm and peaceful presence, but also seems smart as hell. I hope I was right to choose a male therapist this time. I've never been to a third appointment, so I guess so far so good.

He walked into his office ahead of me and I immediately asked, "Can I use the restroom while you take a look at these letters?"

"Sure, it's just down the hall. Can you tell me a little about the letters?" He looked at me with a kind yet quizzical expression.

"Yeah, they were written to me many years ago by the man who had been my gymnastics coach." My voice quivered as I answered.

Raising an eyebrow just slightly, Gary was good at concealing any and all judgment from his expressions.

My heart was racing and I could feel myself starting to sweat. I didn't know what else to say, so I turned and walked down the hall to the bathroom. My palms were sweating, and I was shaking a little...on the inside.

Is this a big deal? God, why am I reacting so physically right now? This was SO MANY years ago? Is THIS why I can't have a functional relationship?

I sat on the toilet, wiped my palms on my skirt, and tried to breath in and out slowly, like I had learned in yoga. Suddenly, my mind went to Justin.

I can't believe I gave the ring back. I can't believe I thought I was going to marry this man, and I gave up. What's wrong with me? Is it that big of a deal if he's not sure he wants to have kids? If I really love him, shouldn't we be able to work that out?

Breathe in, breathe out, breathe in, breathe out. I washed my hands and looked at myself in the mirror.

I weigh 115 pounds. I haven't weighed this since high school. I feel good in my body, but my heart is broken and I don't trust myself. I make shit decisions when it comes to men.

I walked back to Gary's office, and found the door open. I walked in, sat down in the big comfy leather chair, and took my shoes off so I could curl up in a ball.

"Tell me more about these, Torey," he coaxed softly, and with a look of true care and concern.

"Well, when I was fifteen years old, my gymnastics coach kissed me." Tears started welling up in my eyes, but I shakily went on. "I had known for a while that he was sleeping with my friend, Samantha, who was a few years older than me. He talked to me about sex all the time, but after this one meet, where I really screwed up, he kissed me on the mouth. That was just a few months before he moved away from Ohio, but he kissed me several more times before he left." I took a deep breath and tried to slow down. "Then one night, Samantha and I both spent the night at his house, and he kissed us both a lot that night. Those letters were written when he lived in Iowa after he left." I took a deep breath and wiped my eyes with a tissue.

"Torey, I'm so sorry. Someone who you loved and trusted took advantage of you," he said quietly.

Wow! That wasn't the response I expected!

"Tell me again how old you were when this happened?" His eyes were full of care.

"Fifteen," I stammered.

"And how old was he at that time?" Gary's brow was furrowed with concern.

"Thirty, and he was married with a kid." I frowned as all the facts rushed back to me.

"Have you ever told anyone else?" he asked, turning to get a pen and a pad of paper from his desk.

"I told my mom probably ten years ago when I was home from college."

"Did she report it to the police?" he asked matter-of-factly, as if that's what a mom might do.

"No, but she told me she was sorry that happened to me." I choked a little at the thought of my nineteen-year-old self, trying to reach out for validation that Greg was, in fact, way messed up.

"Torey, has anyone ever reported this before?" he prodded.

"You mean like, to the police?" I was surprised at the direction this was going.

I thought he'd just talk to me about how this made me feel.

"Yes, or Child Protective Services?" Gary continued.

"No, not that I know of. You mean this is still reportable, even though he just kissed me and it's been fifteen years?" I asked naively.

"Yes. People who do that kind of thing don't usually stop. I'm going to file a CPS report today. Are you okay to talk more about it now? I need to get some more information from you." He searched my face.

I wasn't quite breaking down, but the tears were flowing. As soon as I walked into this office, the faucets just opened. I could not be in there and not cry.

Poor guy for having to deal with the whole mess of me! My therapist is going to file a CPS report on Greg. Holy shit. Maybe it WAS a big deal? Maybe it is part of why I can't have a successful relationship.

My mind was racing and my stomach was tight, but I pulled it together enough to talk to Gary. "Yeah, I'm okay to talk about it. It's been so long, it's all really kind of surreal to me now; but that's, I think, why I kept those letters…so that I knew I didn't imagine it."

"Torey, it's good that you did. This is really good hard evidence, and if it were ever to come to making a police report, these letters would be very valuable. Okay, now, what was his full name?"

"Gregory Scott Dew." As I said his name, I felt a weird combination of nostalgia and disgust.

"Where did all this take place?" he asked gently. He could tell this was not what I was expecting.

"Ohio. He kissed me at a rest stop somewhere and at a park one time, but mostly it all happened at my gymnastics center and his house."

"And do you know the dates at all?" He leaned forward, gently questioning and nodding as I answered.

"Everything that happened with me, happened in the spring of 1992. He left to go to chiropractic college that summer and I quit gymnastics after we went to Spain to perform in the World's Fair that summer."

"Do you remember the address of the gymnastics center?" he asked.

"Of course, I spent half my childhood there," I said and gave him the name and address.

"I'm sorry, but one more time for the report: how old were you when it happened?" He was taking careful notes.

"I was fifteen." I took a deep breath.

If someone told me this in my office, I would do exactly what he's doing. Why couldn't I apply my own knowledge to myself?

"And how old was he?" he asked again.

"He was thirty." As I spoke the words, it all started to get a little clearer.

What the hell? Greg was sick.

"Do you know where he is or stay in touch with him at all?" His head was tilted with curiosity.

"Yeah, to a degree. I mean, when my parents divorced, I really leaned on him. He was more like a father figure than a coach. As a kid, I totally loved him, but then I found out about Samantha and things just gradually got weirder and weirder. Not only did he talk about sex a lot, but he would tease me about my body and ask to touch my abs; but he was also a mentor and a trusted friend in a lot of ways. He encouraged me to go to chiropractic college and he wrote me a letter of recommendation for PA school when I applied, so that was only about five years ago. He was still in Pennsylvania then, but I'm not sure where he is now. He told both Samantha and I that he had told his wife and gotten help a year or so after he left Ohio, but I've always wondered. I'd hate to hear that he did this to someone else, and I am pretty sure he dated a girl from the gym before Samantha too…so really, I guess it wouldn't surprise me."

"How does all this make you feel, Torey?" Gary asked gently.

Damn you, Gary.

The tears started again. "Sad. I'm just sad. Why couldn't the one guy in my life who I chose to lean on, when I was a kid whose parents divorced, have been a GOOD guy? I mean, in so many ways he was so great. He was part of a place and a sport that taught me the value of hard work, discipline, and dedication. He believed in me when I didn't believe in myself. He told me I was beautiful, and had a great body. I mean, what fifteen-year-old doesn't want to hear that? But, I also knew about Samantha and him, and I didn't really know what to do with that information."

"What did you know about Samantha?" Gary asked when I paused.

"One of my friends told me that Samantha and Greg were together, about two years before he ever kissed me. And Samantha told me herself that they were together, before anything happened with me."

"What did it mean to you that they were together?" He leaned back and folded his hands, shifting his energy from reporter to therapist.

"I assumed that they were together, having sex. They were 'boyfriend/girlfriend' but it was all a secret because of the age difference. Samantha was a little over a year older than me, but that's still more than thirteen years younger than Greg. Samantha and I haven't spoken in years. Last I heard, she was training for the Olympics in pole vaulting."

"Why aren't you in touch?" Gary probed.

"I don't know, I guess it all just seemed too painful. Last time I remember seeing her was at a party in college and she was really upset." I remembered how bad it felt to see her hurting and how I reminded her of that mess.

"Do you want to be friends?" His voice went up expectantly as he asked.

"I don't know. I mean, that life is a long time ago now. I honestly don't keep in touch with anyone from gymnastics at all. I guess I was just ashamed of what had happened and I wanted to forget all of it, so I had to let the good stuff go too? I don't know if it makes any sense, but it was really hard for me to ever go into that gym again. There were just so many disgusting memories there for me."

As I spoke the words, I suddenly realized all the things that I lost when Greg kissed me. So many friendships, so many good times that I had actively tried to stuff away because they were all associated with the shame and guilt that came with those few physical acts.

"But, Torey, you know that implies that you thought it was your fault. And when you are fifteen, it's not possible to give consent to a thirty-year-old coach. He was in a position of authority. He abused his position, and he abused you and Samantha. You did nothing wrong." He spoke slowly and resolutely, maintaining kind eye contact as he said each word.

Tears were just pouring out of me now.

Really? Was it really abuse? Was it HIS fault? Could I have stopped it? Didn't I like the attention? Didn't I write him letters too?

"I guess," I said quietly. I felt like I had just run a marathon and I'd only been in the office for forty minutes. I was exhausted by this conversation. I felt so many different emotions I couldn't even name them, but mostly I was just sad. Sad for my fifteen-year-old self. Sad for Samantha's seventeen-year-old self. Sadness plus shame and guilt, mixed with gratitude and relief, equals what?

Tired and sad. I am tired and sad, and I need some space to deal with all this.

Thankfully, our hour was coming to a close. I took a deep breath and asked the big question: "Gary, do you think that any of this has anything to do with why Justin and I didn't work?"

"Yes, I do. These were some serious infractions on your boundaries when you were still a kid." He smiled gently, knowing I was there to figure some things out and that today we had started to really get somewhere.

"So, I have to work on my boundaries because I didn't know how to deal with this shit when I was a teenager?" I asked hopefully.

"Yeah, something like that. Torey, you know that you can choose who you fall in love with, right?"

I frowned at him. "Not really," I said, feeling as if he had just spoken Latin.

"Well, think about it. If you choose who you hang out with, you can choose who you fall in love with. When you see red flags at the beginning of a relationship, or it just doesn't feel like something good, you should step back a bit. This reflex might not be natural in you because your coach was someone you loved and trusted, but then he hurt you."

I thought for a second, and several situations with past boyfriends flashed through my mind— Brian being with another girl when we met and leading me on, and Justin lying about something important to me. There WERE red flags.

Gary smiled. I think he could tell by the look on my face that something had clicked.

"Torey, what happened with your gymnastics coach was wrong, and it probably does play into your thinking about men and relationships. You're doing the work, Torey. It's going to get better. Looks like our time is up. Do you want to schedule an appointment for two weeks again?"

"Yes, two weeks is great. Same time. Gary, do you think anything will happen with that CPS report?" It made me nervous to think someone might call me, or try to talk to Greg or Samantha about it.

What the hell? A CPS report on ME? Crazy.

"I worked at CPS for a long time, and the number of reports that come in that are present day is high. Something this old will probably get shelved, unless there were other reports. I doubt you have to worry about anything coming out of it anytime soon," Gary assured.

I so want to talk to Samantha now.

"Okay, thanks Gary. I feel a lot better after meeting with you tonight. I think this is good for me. As is yoga. And not drinking."

"Good, Torey. I'm glad. You're doing a lot of good work right now. I'll see you in two weeks."

As I went out to the Subaru, I took a deep breath, and looked up at the beautiful sunset created by, unfortunately, toxic air. I still felt sad and tired, but also somehow just a little bit lighter. I had been carrying a weight of feeling like I was "all f-ed up" and somehow now, I felt the weight lift a little.

Tulare County...This place is so great and so gross all at the same time. Maybe that's kind of like me? I feel so much better after telling Gary about Greg. I didn't realize how much those letters really weighed on me, until I handed them to him. Maybe it's not just me that's messed up? Maybe I never learned how to love right? Poor Justin. I wish I could explain all this to him. I wonder how he's doing? God, I miss him. But, this feels like what I need to be doing right now. I am not numbing myself with alcohol. I am dealing with my shit. I am going to get better. I am going to be good for someone. I am going to get married and have a family someday.

Chapter Sixteen:
Fuming on the Phone

October 26, 2006

I was in the kitchen of the house I had bought right before meeting Justin. I'd lived in this house for more than two years and it really felt like home. The kitchen had an open floor plan with the living and dining room, and the high ceilings made me happy. There was even a wood burning stove that I could use on the rare occasion that it was cold here.

I had been seeing Gary for almost seven months now and so much had happened. I found myself pacing back and forth in bare feet on the cold tile as I listened to the dial tone, pacing under the large and powerful fluorescent kitchen light.

I want my feet on the ground for this conversation.

Ring…… ring…… ring…

"Hello this is Detective Stepuk of the Boardman Police Department," a deep masculine voice said on the other end of the line.

"Hi, this is Torey Votaw," I replied somewhat shakily.

"Hi, Torey. How are you doing tonight?" he asked gently.

"I'm okay. I'm ready to get this over with." Butterflies flittered through my stomach, and my palms began to sweat.

I know that I need to do this. Samantha can't go and confront him. It's going to be okay. But, what if Greg is suspicious of me reaching out to him? What if someone, somehow, told him of

165

our report?

Detective Stepuk's voice helped bring me back out of the chattering inside my brain, "Yeah, I bet. You're going to do fine and it'll all be over soon. He's supposed to call you in about ten minutes, so we have a little time to talk. Do you know how you are going to start the conversation?" His voice was supportive and full of concern.

"Yeah, I mean, I haven't talked to him for several years, but I don't feel worried about being able to. I really do have questions that I want answered, so I think I'll just start as if you weren't even on the phone. I'm going to talk to him about how I can't have a functional relationship. I just called off an engagement, and I wonder if that's partly due to what happened with us…" As I spoke, I felt confident, though I noticed how fast I was talking.

I'm adrenalized already and he hasn't even gotten on the phone yet. This is the right thing to do. If he isn't still acting like this with other women, nothing will come of it, and I won't hurt him in any way. It's just telling the TRUTH. It's just Greg. Greg, who I literally spent years of my life close to. I know he still loves me on some level, and I know he'll talk to me. He's always given me that. If he has gotten help, this will be easy and all good. Nothing but good can come of a conversation for explanation and forgiveness.

"That sounds like a great plan. Just try to remember *not* to be vague. If neither of you mention the actual acts that occurred, it might not be very useful evidence," Detective Stepuk coached me with a gentle tone of guidance that paralleled that of my therapist.

God, I'm glad I have Gary as my therapist now.

I jumped up and down quietly to shake off some adrenaline.

"I understand. I'll ask about Samantha too. When it all happened, that was the one thing that always hung in my head, and made it really wrong—the stuff with Samantha. And, he knew it bothered me, because it made me feel less important to him, so I know I can go there in the conversation." I could hear my voice shaking and my body was doing the same. I was moving constantly, either pacing or doing squats.

166

I need to move my body. Wow, this is just as intense as I could have imagined.

Detective Stepuk continued, "Okay, good. We have a few more minutes, assuming he calls at the right time. Where are you again, Torey?" he asked, lightening the mood a bit and getting my mind off the task at hand.

"I'm in California," I said brightly.

"Nice, do you like it there?" His voiced had changed to one of casual conversation.

"Yes, I do like it. I have both mountains and beach not too far away. I have a good job, a house, and a dog; plus I just started dating a wonderful new guy. I'm happy here. My boyfriend is here tonight too, so I have some support when we get done with this." I smiled, appreciating the comfort of Jay being with me.

"Great. That'll be good for you, but I can already tell that you are a brave and strong woman, or you wouldn't be doing this." He made me blush just a little at his confidence in me.

"Well, thanks. I appreciate that. So, you're just going to be in the background recording all this?" I asked, not sure how a tapped phone call even worked.

"Yes. I'll stop talking as soon as he calls in, and I will be recording. Are you ready?" Detective Stepuk asked one last time as we got close to the call time.

"As ready as I'll ever be." I took a deep breath and did a few more squats, noticing that my stomach was queasy.

Now it's time to just wait.

Waiting, waiting, waiting with the energy of anticipation around me like palpable static, I paced back and forth in my kitchen, trying to quiet my nerves. I did some high knees as silently as possible. In the quiet, my mind flashed through the crazy snapshots of the past six weeks.

Samantha and I reconnecting at Lake Berryessa, riding in a helicopter, playing on boats with nice boys, swimming, drinking in the sun, reminiscing on the good times, and enjoying life. Meeting Jay in Yosemite and climbing with him, laying in El Cap meadow, spraining my ankle, pizza at Degnan's, breaking the dress code at the Awahnee, and then watching "Beautiful Girls," all with this new man.

Where is he?

I walked down the hallway and saw that he was lying on the floor in my room petting Brutus. He looked up at me with his blue eyes and smiled softly as I waved and whispered, "Any minute now." His dark hair and short powerful stature were a source of comfort and support even though I'd only known him for a little over a month.

I'm so glad he's here and has been here through the last few crazy weeks while I dealt with all this shit head on.

I remembered flying back to Ohio and Samantha picking me up. And then the two of us walking into the Boardman Police Department to make our official report to Detective Flara. The campfire at Samantha's, with my old friend from college, Brad. Tears, laughter, hugs, sleep, climbing, work, flights, yoga. So much had happened in the last few weeks, I felt like my life was on fast forward.

It's weird that there are so many good things mixed in with all this shit.

BEEP.... BEEP! I snapped out of my memories and back to the phone.

It's HIM!

"Okay, Detective Stepuk, this is it!" My heart was about to jump out of my chest.

"Good luck, Torey!" He sounded confident that I would do a good job.

"Thanks, here goes," I looked at my phone and pushed the button to answer the call as a three-way.

"Hello?" I said, as strongly as I could muster.

"Torey? It's Greg." He said it with his usual confidence and I could see his face in my mind's eye immediately upon hearing his voice.

No shit. I still know his voice so well.

"Hi. How are you?" I asked, heart pounding, sweating all over, and breathing fast. I paced back and forth on the cool tile.

I can do this.

"I'm well—just driving from my office to home. Can you hear me okay?"

Weird, I can almost hear his smile.

"Yeah, I can hear you fine. So, you are still in Pennsylvania?" I saw a picture of him in my mind, sitting proudly behind the wheel, driving through the rolling hills of southwestern Pennsylvania.

"Yeah, but I go back and forth between two clinics, and we are looking to get back to Ohio permanently. How have you been, T?" he asked with his typical warmness.

"Eh, not horrible, but I've had some thoughts that I am hoping you might be able to shed some light on for me." My stomach was rolling and I kept moving all over the kitchen.

"I'll do my best. I've always wanted what's best for you, T, and for you to be happy. How can I help?" That voice, it may have been years since I heard it, but it's one I could never forget. I had spent so much time with him that I could see his exact facial expressions in my mind as he spoke. This time, though, I was starting to see through his niceties.

"Well…" the tears started rolling down my face and I hadn't even started talking yet. "I just…" *Breathe, Torey.* "…called off an engagement."

At this point, there was a pathetically huge SOB, "and I…"

Breathe in, breathe out. You can do this, Torey.

"I can't seem to have a functional relationship." I spewed the words out like vomit.

Screw this guy. Why am I so weak and vulnerable with him EVEN NOW, fifteen years later? What the hell???

"Ah, I'm so sorry to hear that, T." His deep voice conveyed genuine concern.

I took a deep breath.

That was the hard part. Admitting my failures. I can do this.

I collected myself for a few seconds before continuing. "Well, thanks, but the reason I wanted to talk to you is that…" My voice was shaking a little, but all in all I was doing okay.

You've got this Torey—just say it.

"I think that what happened with us might still be affecting me."

"Okay, well let's talk about it," he said. "I've always felt bad about what happened with us, T. I shouldn't have let it happen."

He has no idea that this is a tapped phone call. He wouldn't be this calm or candid. And what does he mean, "let it happen?" He's the one that made it happen.

"You know, Greg, you were the one stable, loving, good adult in my life; and it just sucks that our coach/gymnast relationship ended with you kissing and touching me. I didn't know what to do with it, so I tried to hang on to the good parts and not the tainted parts, but it just seemed like I could never really separate the two. Eventually, I had to let go of all of it, which is why I haven't been in touch in so long." I wasn't shaking anymore. I was channeling that adrenaline into honesty and anger, and it felt good.

"Yeah, that was just stupid of me. I'm really sorry. I never meant to hurt you. I just thought it might be easier for you to let me go if you were mad at me or hated me." It was amazing that he sounded exactly the same. Not only his tone of voice, but the way he said things.

"What the hell is that supposed to mean? You kissed me to make me hate you? Greg, you were thirty, and I was fifteen. YOU were married and had a kid. You made me part of an adulterous relationship at fifteen. What the hell kind of justification is that— you thought it would make me hate you?" I practically spit the words at him. I could see it and say it clearly now. I wasn't afraid of him anymore. I could call it what it was.

Ha! I just swore at him! I've never sworn around him before! Ha. Mini-win.

"I know it was a bonehead thing to do, but it's what I did at the time. Do you remember what I told you had happened to me when I was eight or nine?" he asked.

It's still so weird hearing his voice after all this time.

170

"You told me something about some babysitter having sex with you or something." I felt kind of gross just speaking the words.

Whatever happened to you doesn't make what you did to Samantha and me alright.

"Well, it was my neighbor, and she was a lot older than me. The details don't matter, but it really affected me."

"I can imagine, and I think the fact that you kissed me and talked to me about sex all the time has really affected me."

"What all do you remember happening with us, T?" he asked quietly.

"I remember the first time you kissed me at the rest stop after that god-awful meet. I remember one time at your house on the couch, at the graduation party, and one time in the aerobics room."

"Only kissing, right? I only ever kissed you," he said with an element of hesitation.

"Yeah, except for the night at your house with Samantha. That night, you had my shirt off too. But, Greg, it's not all about the physical stuff. You made me fall in love with you. You told me things that you shouldn't tell a fifteen-year-old girl on your gymnastics team."

"T, I really cared about you and I still do. I just had a bonehead way of showing it back then." He said it with this convincing apologetic tone that made me want to forgive him.

"It's called sexual abuse" I shot back. *Hell, yeah! I just said that. I'm not going to fall into his charming bullshit.*

"I'm sorry, T," he whispered.

"Well, thanks, for what it's worth. But if you really loved me, what about all that with Samantha—did you love her too?" I asked, knowing that I needed him to share as much information about her as possible.

"Of course, I loved Samantha, but not like you. Samantha pursued me, and I didn't know how to stop it." He was sounding like a teacher again, as if he was telling me what to think.

"Greg, she was only a year older than me, and you were

having sex with her. That's not okay."

"Wait, wait. Samantha and I… we…" He stuttered a moment and then pulled himself together. "I don't know what she told you, but we didn't have intercourse."

"Really? Well, oral sex is sex, too," I said without wavering.

"We never had intercourse and we maybe had oral sex eight or nine times. It wasn't a lot." He spoke the words as if, even now all these years later, he could convince me what was right and wrong. As if he could make me believe what he wanted me to believe.

Screw that. I don't think so.

"But none of it was right, Greg. And I don't know, but I think the way you talked to me and the fact that you kissed me, even when I knew about Samantha, and you were married to Marylou messed me up. It screwed up any boundaries I may have been building. I think that you kissing me, and you having oral sex with Samantha, is all the same messed up stuff that is leading me to not be able to be good in a relationship."

"Well, if it is, I am sorry. That was never my intention. I never meant to hurt you, T." As he said it, the "good Greg" flashed through my brain. The one who told me I was a hard worker and that I deserved good things. I believed him, but I knew by the way he was talking to me, he was still fooling himself about the extent of his behavior.

What am I feeling? A weird part of me actually feels sorry for him. I am sorry that he did this too.

I wished we could go back to those days in the gym and keep all the good things, all the laughter, all the hard work, all the trust, and erase all those creepy things that crossed a very clear but invisible line.

"I've started seeing a therapist and I'm working on it. I just met a guy who is really great, and I'm hoping that by journaling about all this, and getting clear in my head that it was actually a big deal for me, I might be able to do better in this relationship. The other thing that would be helpful to me is to know that you are not still doing this. Has there been anyone since me and

Samantha?"

"No. I promise you." He said it strongly, as if he was convincing himself and not just me.

"No one in Iowa? Or Pennsylvania?" I pushed.

"No, it was only ever just Samantha and you." His tone was somewhat tense and forced, but I was amazed at how his words flowed without hesitation.

"What about Caroline?" I pushed harder.

"Caroline was older than you guys, and I just went to a dance with her," he responded.

That's total bullshit, I thought, but I didn't want to tell him I had talked to her and knew they hadn't just gone to a dance.

"She was still a lot younger than you," I said, trying to show him that I saw a pattern.

"I just went to a dance with her, T. Really."

He's lying. Why is he lying about Caroline? What else is he lying about?

"Well, I'm sure you can imagine why I might wonder. So, you've never kissed any of your patients or cheated on Marylou again after the two of us?" I asked, not holding back my accusatory tone.

"No, never. Really, T. Never again."

"Greg, do you remember what fifty-five meant?" I asked, wondering if his stories were as branded into his memory as mine.

"No, I don't know what you are talking about," he replied quickly.

No further questions, I thought. *We got him with the eight or nine times.*

"Okay, so I can leave this conversation knowing that I am doing my best to heal and take care of myself, and you are not hurting anyone anymore, right?" I asked in the most powerful voice I could muster.

"Yes. I promise, T. I am not hurting anyone. I have four boys now and my life is great. I don't want to hurt anyone. If you need to talk more, I'm happy to do that." I could hear his facial expression, fatherly and knowing.

"I don't think I'll need to, but thanks. Thanks for taking the time to talk to me tonight too." I smiled when I realized I actually meant it. That was one of the most useful conversations I'd had in a long time. He confirmed so many things about himself that I had been questioning. I felt lighter again—still adrenalized, but lighter.

"You're welcome, T. Take care of yourself." As he said the words, I couldn't help but wonder what was going on in his head. This conversation couldn't have been easy for him.

"Thanks, good night." And with that, I hung up the phone.

I heard the click of him hanging up and then quietly asked, "Are you there?"

"I got it all, Torey," Detective Stepuk assured me. "You did great. You got a lot of good information on that call."

"Wow. I can't believe he said that he had oral sex with Samantha eight or nine times. That's about as incriminating as it gets. And he lied about that girl Caroline, too, but at least he admitted some of the stuff about Samantha and me."

"I don't see how it could have gone any better. Good job. Are you going to be alright?" Detective Stepuk asked kindly.

"Yeah. I actually feel pretty good. Like I said, my boyfriend is here and I think we'll just get outside and take the dog for a walk."

"Sounds good. I'll get this to Detective Flara for your file, and I am sure he will be in touch."

"Okay, thanks so much Detective Stepuk. Good night."

When I put the phone down, I felt like I dropped hundreds of pounds.

Whew! I did it. Oh my God, that was crazy.

"I'm done!" I yelled back to Jay.

Jay walked into the kitchen in his plaid shirt and jeans, with Brutus following right behind him. His short stature was inconsistent with the strong, confident, successful, wholehearted, and generally unbelievable man that he was. His confidence was evident in the way he walked, and his bright blue eyes asked if I was okay before he even spoke words.

This man is amazing. I am so lucky to have met him. I am so grateful to have him in my life.

He walked up to me and gave me a huge hug. "How did it go?" he asked as he held me close.

I couldn't believe it, but I was actually feeling really good and alive. I was still a little shaky and sweaty.

Must be the adrenaline.

"Let's take Brutus for a walk and I'll tell you all about it," I said, holding him tight just a little longer.

This is good. Jay is good. My life is good. This is the right thing to do or it wouldn't feel good.

We let go of each other and got Brutus leashed and started out into the cool night holding hands. I felt like I was on a high. It was as if I had just climbed a mountain, or skied a really long run. I felt successful with a huge sense of relief.

I did it!

Jay listened as I told him what Greg had said, and squeezed my hand when I got to the hard parts. Jay was THERE. I'd only known him a few weeks and he was already my rock.

Chapter Seventeen:
Meltdown in the Midwest

Spring 2007

Breathe in, breathe out, breathe in, breathe out. I was so overwhelmed by the amount of new information in the past week, I had to tell myself to breathe.

I had just flown back from Ohio to California the day before, and was back at work. It had been a long day, but it was good to feel like I could help people and give something back. I finished up my last chart and looked out at the Kaweah River running by.

That river is so beautiful, I thought to myself.

It was yoga night and as tired as I was, I knew I needed it. Yoga had become extremely therapeutic and I knew that even when I didn't feel like doing it, it was exactly what I needed. I had a daily home yoga practice in my life, and I knew it grounded me even though it felt too easy.

Why do I always have to beat myself up?

I shut down my computer, checked that the girls didn't need any scripts written or messages answered, and then headed out to my silver Audi A6 wagon to get my mat and yoga clothes. I could hear the river running high, the birds, crickets, and the wind.

I love Three Rivers.

My Audi was fancy with leather interior, an amazing stereo system, a sunroof, and heated seats, but I missed my little Subaru.

Back in January, while driving to work, a man had turned left right in front of me and I'd hit the back end of his truck, immediately bringing me to a stop and totaling my car. The airbag broke my nose, but it could have been way worse. Thankfully, it had been Martin Luther King Day, and Jay was still at my house and came to rescue me. It shook me, but I was back to work two days later.

That was a bad day.

I walked back into the office to change my clothes.

"You going to yoga?", my go-to medical assistant asked. Her brown hair was pulled back in a loose ponytail and her caring eyes said more than her words. Her gentle mannerisms and hard work ethic made her a favorite to both patients and staff.

"Yes. I'm tired, but I need it." I could hear the fatigue in my voice.

"Good. Are you okay?" she asked gently.

"No, but I will be. Thanks for asking. Now get out of here and home to your family," I said with a weak smile.

I walked back into my office and locked the door while I changed my clothes. I put on my black capri yoga pants and a sports bra with my favorite brown "Serenity" t-shirt. That shirt was like a security blanket when I was feeling stressed or shaken, which was, unfortunately, often lately. I put the black dress and heels I had been wearing into my green YGC Shamrocks bag, and slipped on my Teva flip flops.

Ah, comfort. Serenity. Serenity? Not yet, maybe; but it is coming.

I walked back out to the lobby and asked, "You almost done? Let's get out of here."

"I'm getting there, but it was a big day. You saw twenty-six patients. That might be a record for Three Rivers." She smiled and winked at me. We both loved this town and these people.

I smiled back. "They don't like it when I'm gone, do they?"

"No, the fill-in PA never saw more than six a day. When people found out you weren't here, they rescheduled. They all asked about you too. They worry about you."

"That's mutual, but it's time to go home. We can worry

about them all again tomorrow. I'll see you in the morning. And hey, thanks," I looked into her eyes, and I knew that she knew it was for more than just her medical assistant duties. She had supported me through a lot of personal hurt over the last year, and it all just seemed to have come to a head the past week back in Ohio. The hug she gave me this morning was just what I needed. She was a lot more than a medical assistant to me, and I wanted her to know how much I appreciated that.

She looked up from her desk at me knowingly. "Anytime."

That woman is an old soul, I thought as I walked out the door.

It was hot already in Kaweah Country and there were all kinds of lovely Three Rivers sounds surrounding me. Frogs, swallows, the river, crickets, and just an occasional car going by. I threw my bag in the Audi and walked past Anne Lange's and across the street to my yoga studio, Yoga of the Sequoias. As I was walking, I couldn't stop my brain.

I wonder how Dad is right now and how his surgery went today? I wonder what Greg is thinking now and if Samantha is worried that he is out on bail? I don't think he'd ever try to find her or anything, but who knows? What's going to happen with all of this?

It was a few minutes before class started, and I was not that good at sitting quietly, but there was so much in my head that I was thankful for some solitude. I unrolled my mat and sat on my wooden block (handmade by Jay) to "meditate," which I really couldn't do.

I can never slow my brain down and sit quietly.

I tried anyway. I faced the mountain side of the room, adjusted my 'sit bones,' and stretched my spine as much as I could.

I can't even believe everything that has gone on in the past week. Nine days prior, my dad had been life-flighted to Cleveland and could have died. Eight days prior, I had flown to Cleveland to be with him in the hospital; and that same day, though I didn't know it at the time, Detective Flara was interviewing Greg about a patient complaint from his chiropractic office. When he confronted him on the statements Samantha and I had made, Greg confessed. *He confessed! Seriously? It gives me chills just thinking about it.*

Seven days prior, I had awakened on Samantha's couch and Greg's face was above the fold of the local paper with the headline: "Chiropractor Arrested for Sex Crimes."

What are the chances that I would be in Ohio, STAYING WITH SAMANTHA, when Greg was arrested? One in a billion?

Dad was in ICU until just the day before, when I had flown back home.

What the hell? How crazy is it that we made that police report seven months ago and basically heard NOTHING until the day I flew back to Ohio because my dad almost died? This is all too bizarre to not have something to do with the divine. It really feels like a huge abscess of emotion and hurt has erupted. It's hard, but it's also good. Breathe in. Breathe out. Breathe in. Breathe out. Slow down, Torey. It's all going to be okay.

Someone came in quietly and I opened my eyes.

I love this space. I am safe here.

Susan smiled at me. "We missed you last week. How is your dad?" I smiled back at her and at how word travelled fast in this town.

"He's out of ICU, so hopefully on the mend. It's going to be a long road though."

Susan knew a little about the Greg stuff and no one else was there yet, so I figured I should tell her. I was all about full disclosure at this point.

I'm open to help. I need this safe space and the support of these souls.

"My gymnastic coach was arrested the day I flew back, so it's kind of like my whole life blew up in Ohio this past week." As I said it, I felt my heart rate pick up and that familiar pit in my stomach.

"Wow, what does that mean?" she asked, her brow furrowing in concern.

"Susan, I have no idea. He's out on bail, but he admitted to the stuff that happened with Samantha and me. I guess the prosecutor's office has to figure out what's next. There was a woman who came forward with a complaint from his chiropractic office, so that's what led to the questioning. After they finished questioning him about the incident with her, they brought up our reports. The detective told me he was really upset and practically broke down crying and confessed. They arrested him that night. I'm pretty sure more women will be coming forward." I took a deep breath and reminded myself where I was.

"Oh, Torey, this is a lot to deal with all at once. I'm glad you are here tonight. I am holding you in my heart." She placed a hand on her chest as she said it.

Tears welled up in my eyes. "Thanks, Susan. It's so good to be here and have this."

What did I ever do to deserve this place, and these people? Three Rivers is like a little haven of magic for me.

I continued to sit quietly and tried to meditate as some others began to trickle in. I felt the energy of each individual as they entered our sacred space and sat quietly. Some of my favorite yoga friends surrounded me. There was never any music at this yoga class, and I liked it that way. Quiet contemplation in this space, in these poses, had led to important revelations in my mind and my body.

"Good evening, thanks for coming," Susan said quietly. "I'd like to start tonight with a poem by Kay Ryan from her book *Flamingo Watching* called "Leaving Spaces". Susan read the poem slowly and intentionally:

> It takes a courageous
> person to leave spaces
> empty. Certainly any
> artist in the Middle Ages
> felt this timor and quickly
> covered space over
> with griffins, sea serpents,
> herbs and brilliant carpets

of flowers—things pleasant
or unpleasant, no matter.
Of course they were cowards
who liked their swards as
filled with birds as leaves.
All of them believed in
sudden edges and completely
barren patches in the mind,
and they didn't want to
think about them all the time.

Susan quietly closed the book. "Today, let's think about the spaces in our minds and our bodies. Let's think about the way that empty space makes us feel compared to full space or cluttered space, and then let's think about applying that to our minds. Can we clear out space in our mind? How do we do that? How does it make us feel?"

We started into the practice of yoga with Susan leading us gently, but always allowing people to speak or ask questions. This was more of yoga facilitation than what I had always known as a "yoga class," and I had grown to love Susan's style.

If I'm ever a yoga teacher, I'm going to do it like this.

I loved that she encouraged us to speak, ask questions, and offer insights. It was never as if one person was right or wrong in this class; it was all about learning. We'd reference B.K.S. Iyengar's *Light on Yoga* if we couldn't figure something out, and we discussed it.

Yoga had become a very important part of my life, and now that all this shit was blowing up in Ohio, I was so grateful to be in this space, with these people, working on myself, my life, my brain, and my body. Yoga had helped me be more present in so many ways, and allowed me to see that everything doesn't have to be a comparison or competition. There were no scores or grades in yoga. I could do a handstand, but I struggled with a lot of the flexibility poses. It was about gentle effort.

As we fell into a forward bend, I reached my hands clear

182

down below my heels and breathed in and out.

It's amazing how good this feels. Funny that the same pose fifteen years ago in gymnastics was like torture.

My mind flashed back to the feeling of Greg's weight and sweat on my back pushing me into a "pike stretch." Back then, my back rounded into the stretch instead of hinging at the hips.

No wonder it was torture. I didn't know how to do it, and forcing it wasn't helping anything. I never would have thought I'd feel healthier and stronger at thirty, than I did as a gymnast at fifteen, but I'll take it...with a smile.

We were moving through some sun salutations, and I was breathing with the poses. I could feel the presence of my fellow students, and the energy of the room was high.

It's amazing how this movement helps my brain slow down. I can let go of this stuff. It's out of my hands. I can't do anything but love my dad, watch, and wait. I can't do anything about Greg. That wheel was set in motion a long time ago, and he created this mess himself. It's not my mess. Just like my dad created this health mess he is in. It's not my mess either. I can only control myself, and what I do from this day forward. I will try to do my best.

I looked at my feet as I fell into another forward bend, smiling at the twelve-year-old Lorax tattoo on my right foot and the Thai word for "Intent" on my left. I had travelled to Thailand with a friend a few months before to climb. I did as much yoga on the beach as I did climbing, and it was an incredible trip for the end of a painful, yet revolutionary year for me. I finished 2006, my year of sobriety, on incredibly beautiful beaches, doing yoga, climbing phenomenally magical tufas, and snorkeling with new friends and old. I ended the trip getting this tattoo to remind me that the most important thing is not where I end up, but the intent in each individual action.

Even with all this craziness right now, I feel good. I feel grounded. I can handle whatever comes into my space. It seems like Dad will make it out of this; but had he not, I was okay with that. We've had the conversations we needed to have to allow me to forgive. I see him for who he is and I know he loves me. That's always been his intent. I'm still not sure where to put all the Greg stuff in my head, but I feel good about the fact that someone else came forward. Our report never would have gone anywhere if he hadn't continued his behavior. We did the right thing. Breathe in, breathe out. Intent.

Class was coming to an end and I found myself getting comfortable in *Savasana*, the relaxation pose.

Susan's voice was soothing, soft, and wise. "Think back to the poem at the beginning of class. Where do you feel new space in your body? In your mind? Relax your toes. Where can you find more space in your life? Relax your legs. Where can you find more space in relationships? Relax your arms and your shoulders. Where are the spaces you need to focus on? Relax your core. What spaces can you let go?"

I relished the peaceful quiet, and laid there perfectly still, feeling better than I had in the last ten days.

It's amazing how yoga can dissolve my stress.

Savasana always seemed to go by in an instant, and I was slightly surprised to hear Susan's voice again. "When you are ready, allow any movements that feel right." She paused, and gave us the space to take our time. "If and when it feels right, roll to the left, and when you are ready, come to a seated position."

I took a deep breath, rolled over, and pushed myself up with my right hand. I lengthened my back, sitting with my eyes closed, and my hands gently together at my chest.

"With gratitude for the gift of another day, *Namaste*." Susan bowed her head as she closed the class.

"*Namaste*," we all repeated softly.

I felt so much better than I had when I had come into this space. I gathered my things and walked out into the quiet night. The sounds of the river were different at night. As I walked back to the Audi, I thought, *I'm going to be okay. It's all going to be okay. Dad and I are good, and I think he'll pull through this. Greg is not who I thought he was, and he was not honest with me. It's out of my hands. It's out of my control. Live with intent. Intent for good.*

Chapter Eighteen:
Playing in Patagonia

Winter 2008

The bluish haze of the rising sun was showing in the east even though it was only 4 a.m. Jay and I had been hiking for an hour already and were still a few hours from the start of the climb.

We'd been dating for a year and a half and, for the last six months, we had been enjoying the adventure of a lifetime—a year of traveling, rock climbing and, most importantly, no work. We spent the majority of our time in the US, Canada, and Mexico, traveling with Brutus in a small RV, but we had flown to Argentina for a stint in the coveted Patagonia.

The sky was clear and the stars shone brightly over the Fitz Roy and Cerro Torre range.

This place is incredible. I can't believe we've already gotten two summits.

I hadn't wanted to crawl out of my sleeping bag that morning, but once we got going it was easy; we had stashed our packs a few days before when the weather had turned south. The weather was finally looking clear and we were literally down to our last meals, so this was the day to summit San Rafael. It was the third of the "smallest" climbs in this valley, and we had already done the other two. I was a newbie when it came to true Alpinism; but in the four weeks we had been in Argentina, I had done my first Tyrolean traverse over a raging river of glacial run off;

185

donned crampons to walk across a crystal blue glacier that seemed more alive than I would have ever guessed; and enjoyed beers and pizza with some of the world's best climbers in El Chalten. I'd been rock climbing for years, but this was the ultimate adventure in this place I had dreamed about for years.

Content in the early dawn hours, I placed one foot in front of the other through the talus field, on our way up the valley. Jay was a few hundred feet ahead of me, and as I marched on, I let my mind wander to the day we had first met.

I woke up in my tent with a girlfriend of mine, at the snow play area just south of Yosemite Valley. Crawling out of the tent, I was careful not to wake her and grabbed Brutus from the car to take him for a walk. As I walked through the parking lot, I noticed Jay's Saab was parked nearby and the back windshield was covered with stickers.

Hmmm. I haven't been a sticker person for a few years now.

Jay was my friend's friend, and he had arrived sometime in the night. She had flown out from Chicago to meet him and climb for a few days, and she had insisted that I pick her up at the airport and join them for a day of climbing in Yosemite.

I wonder what this guy is like, I thought as I watched Brutus run back and forth, checking out all the new smells. I walked for a while and then headed back to camp when I thought they'd likely be awake. As I came up over the hill to where I could see our camp, I saw him standing behind his car.

Damn, he's too short.

I hiked back toward camp and Brutus, of course, greeted him first. I watched as he leaned down and petted and played with him a bit, and then he looked up and towards me as I walked into camp.

"Hi, I'm Torey." I smiled and held out my hand. "And you've met Brutus."

"Hi, I'm Jay," he said, looking at me with his piercing blue eyes and "living on the road" beard, and shook my hand. "Your dog seems great."

"Thanks! He's my child," I chirped as I opened my Subaru trunk and pulled out my kitchen supplies.

We made small talk as we boiled water for oatmeal. Eventually, my sleepy friend came out of the tent looking rumpled but excited to be out of the big city.

"Let's go climbing!" she exclaimed.

"Eat your oatmeal and we'll pack up and get to the valley," I said, handing her a bowl. I quickly tore down my tent and packed things back into the Subaru with the ease and grace of a seasoned weekend warrior. She and I jumped in my car, and Jay followed us in his down to the valley.

An hour or so later, I was standing in the sun next to him. "How long are you here for?" I asked, as we began to set up shop on Pine Line at the base of El Cap for an easy single pitch climb for beginners.

"I'm not sure. Maybe three or four weeks. My parents live down by L.A., so I'll go see them for a while after I finish up here." Jay was flaking the rope out and I was finding a harness for one of our friends to use; and I noticed that his small frame was muscular and competent, and that he did everything with precision and grace.

"Nice. I heard you are going to climb El Cap. Who are you climbing with and what route are you taking?" I hoped to hear more about his adventure.

"I'm going to solo Triple Direct," he said it without hesitation, as if it had already happened.

Who IS this guy?

"Let me get this straight. This is your first time in Yosemite Valley, and you are going to SOLO El Cap?" I didn't even try to hide my awe as I got geared up to set a top rope on Pine Line.

"Yep." He looked down. He clearly wasn't trying to impress me; he was just stating a fact.

"That's crazy."

"Why?" he asked.

Because I don't think I could ever do that. Because people talk about El Cap like it's the final frontier. Because I've seen SO MANY competent climbers get their asses kicked on El Cap WITH a partner. Because people train all year to do El Cap. Because holy shit, is that ballsy?

"It's kind of big deal to climb it at all, let alone by yourself." I smiled.

Holy shit! Really, who IS this guy?

"It'll be fine; it's just aid climbing."

JUST aid climbing? This guy is unreal.

The confidence this short Wisconsin man had was unbelievable. He was so modest, yet so real. A far cry from the guys who tout all their accomplishments or spew about what they're going to do. He was just nonchalantly stating that he would solo El Cap as if it was already a fact.

This dude is amazing, but it's only been six months since Justin and I broke up. I cannot date another climber from Wisconsin. My luck, they probably know each other.

We climbed all day together and did a few routes that the others who were with us couldn't do. Swapping leads, it was obvious we'd make good free climbing partners. As we climbed, we talked and talked about where he grew up and what he wanted in life.

"What's it like to be a chemical engineer?" I asked, feeling at ease and wanting to know more about this man.

"I was in a research position at the University of Tulsa for the past two years, but I'm not sure I like it. I think I might want to go back to med school or PA school. But I do know that I want to get to Colorado again, and I want a house and a family."

I am intrigued.

"I am a PA," I said. "It's got its perks, but if you have a master's degree in engineering, I don't think I'd recommend going back to PA school. I bought a house a couple years ago and I love it, but I want to get married and have kids too. I'm in the midst of processing some pretty heavy stuff from my childhood, and then I am hopefully going to be a datable person again."

Wow, I said that pretty quick. I hope I don't freak him out.
"What do you mean?" He turned toward me, his blue eyes looking directly into mine.

Deep breath, my heart rate picking up a little at his intense gaze.

"My gymnastics coach was a douchebag, and next weekend I am flying back to Ohio to make a police report against him." I tried to say it as matter-of-factly as I could, but the truth was that I was kinda freaking out on the inside about it.

"Wow. That can't be easy," he said with raised brows as he tied his figure eight.

Thank you! Thank you for not saying you're sorry.

I put Jay on belay and he looked at the rock in front of him.

"No, it's not, but last weekend I had the amazing opportunity to reconnect with an old friend who is going to report with me. I think it makes it SO much easier since there are two of us that were both involved. We witnessed each other's abuse, so we can support one another. Last weekend, we met up in Northern California on a lake with some great guys who treated us like queens. We flew in a helicopter and played on boats. We hardly even spoke of the situation we are about to face, and it was good. We played hard, just like we did when we were kids." I couldn't help but smile thinking about dancing on the front of the boat with Samantha at 3 a.m.

Jay just listened as he gazed at the rock in front of him. He heard me, and he didn't run.

"That's brave of you both." He paused and looked at me with wide eyes.

"Thanks, you're on belay when you're ready." My stomach was a little queasy thinking about what lay ahead, but I was amazed to be able to talk so openly about it with Jay.

"Climbing," he said.

"Climb on," I responded and watched as he and started up the crack system.

Later that night, I was standing around the fire at Camp 4 where he and the rest of that crew were staying. Brutus was with me and we were going back to my friend's house instead of camping with them. I had to take off in the morning to volunteer at another climbing event, so I was circling the fire saying my goodbyes.

When I came to Jay, I searched for the right words—a way to tell him that I'd like to stay in touch.

"Hey, since you are going to be here for a few more weeks, would you want a weekend climbing partner in two weeks?" I asked hopefully.

"Sure. That'd be great. You've never aid climbed, right?" His blue eyes twinkled.

"Not really, but I'd love to learn," I said, feeling hopeful and excited.

"Do you want to do Washington Column in two weeks?" he inquired.

"I love that plan. It's been on my list for a while. Of course, I can't guarantee that I'll be great company based on what I have coming up next week, but I'd love to climb with you." It was so easy to be sincere and truthful with this guy.

"It's a plan then," Jay said, as he pulled his phone from his pocket to get my number.

I smiled as I gave it to him.

Sweet. Washington Column with this guy.

"Okay, I think I need to head back to my friend's and go to bed. I am meeting my local climbing group for a volunteer event at 10 a.m. tomorrow in Sequoia." I thought that was a good cue for a hug, but he didn't make any move to hug me. He just nodded at me, so I turned and headed into the night.

Weird. All day, I thought that guy might be kind of interested...but no hug?

An icefall across the valley brought me back to the path I was following in Fitz Roy Valley. I stopped and turned to watch the waterfall of snow and ice crash down the side of the mountain a mile or so away.

Powerful. This place is always changing. I can't believe it's been just over a year since we met.

I glanced at Jay who had also stopped to watch the icefall and was just below the ice field that we had to navigate. I caught up to him and sat down to pull my crampons out of my mini pack.

"That was big," I said to him, gesturing toward the ice fall.

"Yeah, I think that may have been the biggest one since we've been here. We made good time getting up here. How are you feeling?" he asked with a smile.

"Great. I'm finally getting used to this place and it's going to be time to move on." I was comfortable and confident today. I felt great.

"Maybe, but next is Bariloche—climbing towers in the sun with pizza available nearby. Nothing bad about that," he said with a hint of longing.

"Agreed." I was stuffing a granola bar in my mouth as I re-laced my blue La Sportiva mountaineering boots. When I had been moving, I was warm, but sitting still for just a few minutes had made me cold. Maybe it was from looking at the field of ice we were about to enter.

"Let's get going," I said, a hint of my uneasiness about ice travel racing back into my mind.

"Okay. Just remember to keep your ice ax ready and kick little steps as you walk at a gradual angle. You'll be fine. I'm right behind you," Jay assured me. He was much more experienced than I was in this world.

I started off somewhat apprehensively and he followed behind. As I kicked my crampon into the ice, I started to see that the ice was much harder than it had been the other day when we were up here. I had to kick harder and sometimes twice, and I wasn't moving as fast as I had before, because I didn't like the way the ice felt. Jay had more weight than me, and more force, and he was staying pretty close behind me. I focused on my technique and plodded on.

Thirty minutes or so had gone by, and we were close to the

top of the ice field. Jay was just 10 yards or so below me on the other side of the field. The sun was shining bright and warm, but the wind was kicking up a bit. Jay was moving faster, getting closer to me. I refocused on my steps and kept moving.

Almost done. This ice creeps me out.

My heart nearly jumped out of my chest the moment I heard Jay yell. I looked down to see that he had fallen and was sliding down the ice. But somehow, the next thing I knew, his body was upright and his feet were running across the ice. He was up. He was okay.

Jesus! My heart was racing and I was almost nauseated with the thought of *"what if?"*

I moved as quickly as I could to him. "Are you okay?" I yelled to him. He waved at me but didn't say anything. He had slowly made his way off the ice and was sitting in the boulder field.

It probably only took me two minutes to get to him, but it seemed like forever.

"Are you okay?" I asked again frantically.

"Yeah," he said casually.

I kissed his bearded cheek and gave him a hug. He leaned on me, but didn't hug me back. As I pulled away and looked at him, I noticed that his eyes weren't focused and he was breathing more slowly than I expected.

Shit! What's wrong?

I sat down and grabbed his scraped hands and started checking him out.

"Did you hit your head?" I asked as I squeezed each hand and tried to assess if he was physically hurt or just in shock. I ran my hands over his body, checking for pain or blood.

"I don't think so," he said quietly, and I realized he was about to pass out.

"Jay, stay with me," I yelled as I pinched the part of his hand between his thumb and forefinger. He took a deep breath and that seemed to pull him back. I kept looking for injuries as he seemed to collect himself and get some blood back to his brain.

"Wow. Okay. I'm okay," he said, looking surprised, as if he wasn't sure how he got there. He breathed deeply again, and I could see his focus come back to him.

Whew. Holy shit! Was that scary!

I sat down next to him and put my arms around him, the gravity of the possibilities settling into my mind.

"That could have been horrible." I glanced over at the five hundred yards of forty-degree ice that led to a pile of huge boulders. "You could have died." I didn't even want to think about it. I was so grateful to be sitting next to him, just holding him.

I love this man. He's my forever guy.

Jay hugged me back and, as he shook off the experience, started reassuring me. "Torey, I'm okay. I'm not even sure what happened or how I got my feet under me again, but I am okay."

We took a little time to eat some food and drink some water. When he seemed completely normal, we pressed on to the summit of Aguja Rafael.

Six hours later, we found ourselves at the start of the last pitch. Huddled behind a boulder on the ledge, looking over at the immense beauty of the Fitz Roy, the wind was howling. We could barely hear each other, even just a few feet away from one another, if we weren't protected by the boulder.

There's only one pitch left. We should try to summit, but I hate this wind.

Jay was determined to get to the top, so he started out to lead the last pitch. The start of the pitch was easy, but then it moved into thin 5.10 or harder rock climbing.

This isn't going to be easy.

He got midway up the vertical thin section and, with gusts of wind probably fifty miles per hour, he was practically being blown off the wall. Wisely yet reluctantly, he decided we'd climbed high enough for the day.

I belayed him back to me, and when he got close enough for me to hear him, he said, "It's not worth it."

"I agree. It's just way too windy. It's been a good day, and I want to keep you safe." I shook my head at the memory of the morning slide.

"Yeah, let's just sit here for a bit and then we can start rapping down." Jay cuddled in next to me behind the boulder, and we peeked out at the glorious mountains across from us. We'd been moving for about twelve hours already, and the reality was that we were only half way done.

I love this man. My life will be an absolute adventure with him. I know we'll get married. He's been with me through so much and he's so understanding. I really don't want to go across that ice field at night.

"Let's get moving. I'm getting cold," I said with a shiver at the thought of what was ahead.

"Okay," he said. "The rap should be pretty quick." Jay started reorganizing gear and I flaked out the rope. We had been climbing so much together at this point that no words were needed. We both knew what to do and before long we were at the bottom of the route and on "flat" ground again.

Thankfully, when we got to the ice field, it was still soft from the sunny day. The wind had died down, and we were protected a bit since we were lower. Despite my fears, we made it across the ice without incident.

As we scurried down over boulders big and small, I felt overwhelmed with the immense gratitude I felt for this man. I don't know what I would have done if he would have slid down that ice field and been hurt. He'd been "with" me from the day we met. He listened patiently to me tell the crazy story of going to the police about Greg on our first date on Washington Column; and my mind was so wrapped up in that experience that it was all he heard about for the first few weeks of us dating. Then he came to my house and was there when I did the tapped phone call. He was willing to give me the time and space I needed to let him into my life, and my heart was full of love for him.

I'm going to marry this one.

My mind flashed back to going home after that first weekend with him and Googling his name. I smiled at the thought of what I had found.

He's so humble. He's so smart and competent. He's such a good guy. THIS is my husband.

The sun was going down and the alpine glow on the Fitz Roy was insane. The mountains were literally glowing pink and the white glaciers presented a beautiful contrast. We were still a few hours from our high camp, and I knew it was going to get cold. This was a big day, but we only had breakfast left at camp, so that meant we had a six-mile hike, with all our gear, the next day to get back to our base camp and a stash of food. I was tired, but I loved that feeling of utter exhaustion even if we didn't get a summit.

I love my life. I love this man. There's a trial in my future, but my life is so good now. I feel like I could handle just about anything.

Chapter Nineteen:
Crazy in the Courtroom

March 31, 2008

"All rise," the bailiff said, and I stood up with everyone else in the courtroom.

Samantha was standing to my left, and one of the other victims was on my right. Samantha reached out and grabbed my hand, and I extended the same to the woman next to me. All of us stood hand in hand in the front row of a courtroom stocked to the gills with people supporting Greg, not us. My palms were sweating, and my heart was racing.

We have already won. They found him guilty. There is NO WAY, after all this, that he won't get more than the four years he could have taken in the plea deal. I don't get it. Why didn't he just take the plea?

The door opened, and Judge Krichbaum walked into the courtroom.

"Good morning," he said with his brisk authoritarian tenor.

I like this guy, I thought as he sat down and cleared his throat.

We all sat down, but kept holding hands.

Natasha Frenchko, our badass prosecuting attorney, stood up and stated we were all here for the sentencing of "The State of Ohio vs. Greg Dew." Her stylish long brown hair, makeup, and clothes spoke to her professionalism, but they didn't reveal the ferocity that lay beneath. She read the case numbers and the numbers of all the violations of which he was found guilty on the Friday before, though there were many he was found not guilty on too. The list of guilty convictions was long. Three counts of rape for Samantha, as well as a count of Corruption of a Minor. One count of Rape for a chiropractic patient, one count of Gross Sexual Imposition for me, as well as one count of Gross Sexual Imposition for another chiropractic patient. Felony of the first degree, violation, felony of the third degree, violation.

Violation...yes...so many...

That word, VIOLATION, was repeated over and over.

I guess maybe it was a big deal, Greg. Maybe you should have taken the plea. Who ARE you? I didn't see any of the "good" you this past week. I just saw a LIAR. Natasha was right.

I thought back to that day, just over a week prior, while I was prepping for the trial with her.

Natasha was sitting across from me at a small table, with a steno pad and two folders of evidence against Greg, each about five inches thick. She was going over the evidence, and asking me some of the questions that she planned to ask me on the stand, so that I'd know what to expect.

I was nervous then, just as I am now, I thought. *Maybe I've been nervous for a long time.*

Then she asked me the question that changed my life forever. It was just a question on her list, along with "Where do you live? And what is your profession?"

"What made you think he would talk to you when you made the tapped phone call?" she inquired.

I didn't even hesitate. The answer spewed out. "I knew he still loved me and respected me enough to talk to me."

Natasha's jaw dropped, and her eyes popped like a cartoon character and she responded flatly, "Torey, he never loved you or respected you."

My whole brain screeched to a stop.

What? Really? Wait, wait.

Sixteen years flashed by in an instant and I became truly present to THAT ONE MOMENT.

She's right. Oh my God. It's so clear now, it's almost comical. My poor little fifteen-year-old brain didn't know how to separate the good from the bad, and wanted SO BADLY to hold on to the good, that my brain had made it okay. I made the bad "no big deal" in my head. Sure, he did something wrong, but he still loved me and respected me.

"Oh, my God! Natasha, you're right! I'm about to testify against this guy in a criminal trial and there's a piece of me that still thinks he loves me. And that makes it hard. But you're right. He doesn't love me. He doesn't respect me. He's a predator."

I immediately felt lighter. It was as if that one realization was the missing piece that was going to allow me to actually follow through in the courtroom. I could get up on that stand, feeling no conflict in my heart that this was the right thing to do.

He never loved me or respected me. I can own that.

Natasha's voice brought me back to the courtroom and the sentencing again: "Ten years for each Rape count and eighteen months for each Gross Sexual Imposition charge for a total of forty-three years. We have zero days credit for time served calculated. And prior to the court imposing sentencing, the four victims for the counts for which he was found guilty would like to make a statement."

The chiropractic patients were the first to make statements. Judge Krichbaum was very direct and kind of a hardass to everyone, not just the felon in the courtroom.

I bet the fledgling attorneys learn a lot from him and appreciate him, even if he is a ball buster.

I listened with one ear as the other women spoke, but also read through my statement one last time. I was speaking for myself, but also for Samantha because I knew she wasn't going to speak for herself. As the second victim finished, she thanked the Court for its time and consideration, and I knew I was up. I held the statement I had typed on my stepdad's computer over the weekend in my hand, and stepped up to the podium.

"Good afternoon…" Judge Krichbaum said.

"Good afternoon," I started, with a glitch in my voice that sounded weak.

Dammit, Torey, do this right. Be strong. I can say this now. No questions, no cross examination.

I gathered myself and plowed on, "Your honor, the defendant is a sexual predator and he should not be allowed in public. I believe that he has most likely impacted ten times as many individuals as those who have come forward, and I think that he should not be allowed access to any possible innocent victims again…"

I paused to breathe and try to shake the nausea from my stomach.

"Part of the reason he is so dangerous is that he fools so many people into believing that what he does is okay, apparently even his wife. Since the summer of 1992, when the defendant left this area and ceased to be in the position of my coach, I have been trying to put these crimes behind me. I have had a hard time trusting men…"

Ugh, my chest felt tight and I hated to even say this out loud, but I needed to be honest about the impact.

"And although I have known for many years that what he did was wrong, I held on to ideas that he implanted when I was a child. Even as I met with Natasha Frenchko last week, I referred to the defendant with terms of respect and love and thinking that he still had these for me. This past week has been more stressful than I could ever imagine. I never would have thought that Miss Kelley would have asked some of the questions that she did, and I do realize that these questions were fueled by his fiction. The disrespect that was shown to us as victims as well as the disrespect and mudslinging that was targeted at our families appall me. I can't imagine that less than two weeks ago I mentioned the words love and respect in reference to Greg Dew..."

Saying his name felt good, even though it almost got caught in my throat. He was right next to me as I read my statement, and I could feel his eyes on me.

This is so surreal.

I kept on reading as clearly as I could: "He had the audacity to get up and tell endless lies while under oath, and at the same time continually referring to his faith and strength in God and the depth of his religious views. He has shown no remorse even for the incident that he took minimal responsibility for, and continues to deny many acts he had admitted to previously. He knows the truth and he has sculpted it, reworded it, and morphed it into a mess, an unspeakable mess, to try to keep the veil of secrets over his wife, his children, his extended family, and even his religious friends..."

I paused and took a deep breath. My body felt shaky, but my voice had sounded strong and clear so far.

Whew, I'm doing this. Keep going, Torey. You have to stick this landing.

"At this point I have no desire to be looked on as a victim. At the age of fifteen I was a victim, and yes, this man had a negative impact on my life. Now, however, I am a strong and independent woman who is trying to protect other people and assist a friend who needs to heal.

"The true victims of this man's life are now his children, and I truly believe his sons would be better off without him as the prominent male in their lives. I can only hope he has not taught his sons that this type of behavior is acceptable. I hope they have not learned the subtle ways that he has controlled people. I hope they have been in counseling.

"Lastly, I hope that this trial is a—this year and a half of denial has not cost his family a huge amount of money that could have helped them in the future. Thank you."

I finished reading my words and immediately wished I could go run out of the courtroom and around the block.

I did it. That felt okay. I feel stressed, but strong.

"All right. Thank you," Judge Krichbaum said as I went

back to the bench and sat down next to Samantha. He called her name, but she just shook her head.

"All right. Let the record show that Miss ███████ does not wish to address the court."

Okay, it's their turn now. I wonder how this is going to go.
His lawyer stood and started talking.

"…Virtually everyone in this courtroom today, with the exception of the people seated in the front row of the court's right-hand side, are in the support of Dr. Dew."

Well, that's true, I thought. *At least some things she says are true. I still can't believe any woman in her right mind would defend him with the evidence available.*

She picked up a two-inch-thick stack of papers and continued, "I have received this stack of letters which I would like to have made a part of the record for the sentencing."

Judge Krichbaum said, "Very well, the court will accept them as part of the record for sentencing."

She proceeded, "Your honor, Dr. Dew throws himself on the mercy of the court today. We would ask this court to impose as little prison time as the statute will allow. Although we are very sensitive to the fact that the court is obligated upon a conviction to punish the offender, we would also like to point out for the court that every single day that Dr. Dew is away from his family, his friends, and his supporters constitutes punishment for them."

What the hell? Maybe it constitutes SAFETY for them, not "punishment." I shifted in my seat, trying to manage my frustration.

His lawyer went on to say that there were people that would like to address the court on his behalf.

His mom spoke of him as the "fruit of her loins" and "one that I suckled at my breast" and then she thanked God for him. None of that surprised me, but it started getting a little weird when she said, "He stands before you in orange today, but that is not his color. His color is purple, the color of royalty for he is a king among men."

What does that even mean? He's not a king among men;

he's a pedophile. Maybe this is why he has the audacity to even fight this in court, because his mom's been telling him he's a king all his life.

She finished her statement, "May God bless us and especially Greg and his family as we are all hollow without him."

Now *that*, I understand. I felt a pit in my stomach and remembered how I felt when he left for Iowa...empty.

He can make you feel like that, like you NEED him. It's so crazy.

His younger brother spoke next. Samantha and I had known him when Greg was our coach. Since he was a few years younger than Greg, closer to our age, he was around now and then. I seem to remember Greg trying to set Samantha up on a date with him.

Weird. This whole thing is just bizarre. My head hurts.

It was bizarre to see him stand up there and almost immediately start referencing the Bible. "In the Old Testament, we can read and come to some kind of understanding of a judge, much like unto yourself, when we read of King Solomon. When accepting his call from God to be a judge unto the people, King Solomon was thankful to God for the great mercy he had shown his father, King David. God granted this mercy onto David because of his adherence to truth, righteousness, and uprightness of heart, and Solomon followed in his father's footsteps... We stand united before you on this day, March 31, 2008, and ask that God will grant unto you an understanding and discerning heart to judge our brother, son, uncle, or father, Gregory Scott Dew... We ask that you might follow King David and King Solomon's example and exude adherence to truth, righteousness, and uprightness of heart as to what you have experienced during this court proceeding... May God bless you and inspire you in regard to this matter. Sincerely, ███████████."

My heart was racing, and my palms were sweating. It was hard not to roll my eyes or laugh during some of this, but I knew that would not be appreciated in the courtroom.

All this Bible quoting on his behalf is killing me. God doesn't want grown men trying to have sex with little girls. It's

NOT OKAY. What the hell? Deep breath, Torey. What's going to happen next? This is beyond bat shit.

Next up, a man from his church, apparently his bishop. The bishop, who referred to him as "Brother Dew" went on to describe how Greg had saved a little boy who fell into a pool and was drowning.

So, am I following that that means you believe that if you save a life, it's okay to molest girls and women? Is that how it works in your church?

He went on about how great a guy Greg was, and all the good work he had done in his life, and how much his sons needed him.

I don't think so!

And then, much sooner than I would have expected, he was done.

Funny that the bishop didn't reference the Bible at all.

I watched the bishop take his seat and looked around for the next person to stand.

Ugh, this is taking forever. I'm SO READY to be done with this. Last week was a whole week of feeling like I'd run a marathon after every day in this courtroom. I'm so ready to be done with this and done hearing about what a great guy Greg is even after he has been found guilty, for God's sake.

His pricy Cleveland female lawyer went on to talk about his "sterling reputation in the community." Then she went on to say that, "Greg will not be giving the court what the court might interpret as a traditional statement of remorse. He respects the court. He respects the jury's finding, but he is planning on appealing this case. And in order not to endanger his future claims on appeal or any post-conviction matters, he does not want to say something inappropriate. However, he will express to the court that he and his family do feel badly for the pain and the violations which the victims sincerely believe happened to them."

Well, okay. What is that? Is that "lawyer speak" for he's not going to say he is sorry because he's been denying that any of this happened? Oh wait, except for when he confessed to the police, and when he talked to me on the tapped phone call. Ugh. This is both physically and mentally exhausting.

I glanced over at him, noticing the "holier than thou" expression on his face.

Why didn't he just take the plea? Why did he want the trial? He knows he did it. He knows he's guilty. It's all just a game now. I wonder if it's something about getting to heaven? Maybe there's some religious law that says if you admit your wrongdoings, you can't get through the pearly gates? Wear the magic underwear, don't smoke, don't swear, don't drink alcohol, and don't admit you are a pedophile (even if you are) and then you can get through the pearly gates.

I saw him sit forward.

Alright, here it comes. He's up.

Greg stood up and approached the podium. He was wearing orange prison garb and three days of stubble. He looked old. He held his head high as always. There was not a single inkling of remorse on him.

"Thank you, Your Honor. I would first like to start off by expressing my gratitude and love to my family and everyone in the courtroom who has shown me love and support throughout this trying time in my life. With that said, I would also like to express my gratitude for each one of the people listed on the indictment who said at some point in their life that I was helpful to them. I also understand the graveness of the allegations that are made against me and the pain and suffering that they said were caused by my actions. I truly hope that through the results of the court the verdicts that were handed down, that they can receive some type of closure, and I pray that they can receive relief and peace in their lives because of that."

I felt nauseous.

That's an interestingly sneaky and half-assed apology, but thanks for praying for me, Greg. I'll find my peace.

"I am also—I would like to express my gratitude to the jury and my great respect for them. I believe that they were very merciful at the time when they dismissed the vast majority of the

charges that were charged against me. I also believe that they did
the best they could and were very thoughtful in their deliberations
with the information they had presented to them, as well, and I
respect them for that. I would also like to express my great respect
for this court, for you as the Judge over this proceeding. I have
always tried to adhere to whatever the court has asked me to do,
shown up on time, been appropriate. I apologize for not shaving.
They wouldn't let me shave. I did not have access to that, but I do
show that respect to you, as well, Your Honor."

C'mon, does he want pity? Please. I shifted in my seat again
and held onto the arms of the chair, partially to stabilize me and
partially to keep me from jumping up and laughing in his face.

"In light of that, I do ask for your mercy, Your honor. My—
although I have been found guilty of these things, I still would like
to maintain that it has never been my intention to hurt anybody in
my entire life. Hopefully the amount of people that are here and
the hundreds of people who have contacted me throughout this
thing are proof that I have done more good in my life than I have
ever done bad. Again, Your Honor, like my attorney said, in the
future I am going to express my – try to exercise my right to
appeal. So I will just leave my comments, again plead for mercy of
the court on sentencing, Your Honor. Thank you." He stayed
standing at the podium looking like a convict.

*Okay, It's Judge Krichbaum's turn. He's always seemed
thoughtful and wise. I wonder what he'll have to say here?*

Judge Krichbaum took a deep breath and rocked back in his
seat just a bit. He was the classic picture of a Judge in court, as he
looked at Greg. "Well, I remarked during the week as long as I
have been here I don't know that I've ever seen such a show of
support for a defendant. You certainly do have a lot of people who
like and admire you."

"Thank you," Greg replied.

The Judge continued, "In fact, I was criticized publicly
because I wrote a letter on behalf of a criminal defendant once, and
the criticism, of course, was born out of ignorance on the part of
the media who printed it because you can't be a judge, you can't

be fair unless you consider all that there is to the person, not just the bad things, but if there are some good things to say about that person too. I don't know how anyone could judge another without opening the doors to any information about the person that you could give me. So that certainly impresses me.

"I have two sons. They mean the whole world to me, and the thought of ever being taken away from my family is a – is a pain that even thinking about it is very difficult to endure. A situation like that, though, is one that I tell people all the time when they come here and tell me think about my family, think about how hard this is on them, think about my children being without me. You have to remember something as a theme throughout this whole situation. I didn't do this to you. I didn't bring this about. And whatever the sentence is going to be is not something that I am going to do to you. It's something that you did to you.

"This case was discussed when it began, and before this trial that you were offered a generous plea agreement where your time could have been minimized, and you chose to reject it. That's a decision that you have to make. It's a decision that you have to live by. The danger with rejecting a generous plea bargain, and offer of a sentence that was presented to you is that that once we go to trial, then I learn all the things that the state wants to say about you. I don't know those things before the trial. But once we go to trial, I certainly know the things that you're accused of doing and that the jury found beyond a reasonable doubt that you did. And so I view the case a whole lot differently. And in a situation like this, I have to look at what you were charged with, what you were convicted of, and the gravity of these offenses, and certainly the effect, what these types of crimes have on the victims.

"I can't help but analogize this to a book I read. It's called *QB VII* by a fellow named Leon Uris. It's about a doctor who was a gifted doctor who was employed by the Nazis in World War II to commit the atrocious medical acts against the human guinea pigs in a concentration camp. And he was forced into that, but he continued to do it and began to actually excel at it. He escaped from that concentration camp and took on a mission in his life to do good where he actually went to foreign countries and improved their lot and served for minimal amounts of money and cured and healed and helped everyone who he ever came across, sort of as an atonement for his earlier crimes. He got to be such a great humanitarian that he was Knighted by the Queen of England. And when an author began to research Nazi war crimes, he included this Dr. Adam Kelno in his book and described all the God-awful things he had done. This guy got to the point where he thought he was above all of that, where he was—that that wasn't him. That was someone else because he had done all these wonderful things and the wonderful things outweighed the horrible things that he had done. So he sued the author of the book, and pretty much the whole book is about the trial that took place in the English court. When it was over, the jury found in favor of the doctor and awarded him one penny for the damage that had been done to his reputation.

"I suppose I use that analogy in thinking about this because I certainly do believe that you have touched many, many lives very positively, that there is good in you. But you have also done some God-awful things in your life. Beyond any reasonable doubt you did horrible things to these little girls at a time when they didn't know any better, and you certainly did know better. And then, to abuse patients who come to you for help, put their trust in you and their faith in you, and to engage in the conduct you did with them is just unforgivable.

"So there is two sides to your personality, two sides to who you are. And, as your brother said, you know, I pray, too. You know, I would love to be as wise as Solomon, and I would love to be perfect in my judgment. In fact, I strive to be perfect in my judgment. But what all the folks in this courtroom got to hear, and, in fact because you filed a Motion to Suppress the statement that you gave the police, I got to see on the videotape was your confession to these acts. And I have to tell you, it was bizarre to see and hear all those things in the confession and then have you take the witness stand and it was like it never happened. To me it validated what these young ladies said about you and your personality.

"I thought a lot about this since your conviction, and, certainly, I agree with you, the jury couldn't have been more fair and more attendant to their duty. They found you not guilty of more things than they found you guilty of. And from the time that they took and the effort that they employed, it's pretty obvious they went through each and every shred of evidence on each and every one of these charges before they made the unanimous decisions that they made on each and every one of the verdicts.

"So I am satisfied that justice was served and that you received a fair trial, and I, too, respect the verdict of the jury. In that regard and in thinking about it, I just have to tell you that I have always been of the philosophy, and can't escape it, that I don't give discounts for multiple crimes. I just can't see that as appropriate, that the more crimes you commit, the less the penalty, that concurrent sentences don't address each and every one of these wrongs. Each and every one of these wrongs has to be addressed. I think to do anything other than that is a bad message to give others who would even imagine doing something like this. Everybody needs to know that this is something that is going to be dealt with appropriately by the courts in this community.

"The court has to consider the purposes and principles of sentencing under 2929.11, those being to punish the offender and to protect the public from future crimes by you and by others like you. The court is to consider the need for incapacitation, deterrence, rehabilitation, and restitution. The sentence is to be commensurate with and not demeaning to the seriousness of your conduct and its impact of the victims and must be consistent with sentences for similar crimes by similar offenders. The sentence is not to be based on your race, ethnicity, gender, or religion."

Judge Krichbaum is great. I'm so thankful he was assigned to our case.

Knowing we were in good hands, I took a huge breath and felt a bit of my tension release.

"Factors that make the crimes more serious, the injuries exacerbated by the victim's physical condition at the time, both with the gymnasts and with the patients. The victims have testified to and established that they have suffered serious psychological harm. You held a position of trust with these persons and abused that position. Your relationship with the victims facilitated each and every one of these offenses.

"Factors that make the crimes less serious are inapplicable.

"Factors that make recidivism more likely. My understanding is that you have no prior criminal record or juvenile record, but you show absolutely no remorse.

"Factors that make recidivism less likely, you have no prior juvenile record or adult record, so it appears that the recidivism factors balance out.

"The court next considers the considerations in 2929.13 regarding felony sentencing. I have to consider all the things that I learned at the trial, all the things that the victims had to say, and all the things that you told the police and you told Miss Votaw over the telephone and then denied when you took the stand.

"So it is the sentence of this court that for the crime of rape in Count One in the Case 07 CR 378, you should be taken from here to the Mahoning County Justice Center and from there to the Department of Rehabilitation and Corrections, there to serve a term of ten years and to pay the costs of prosecution.

"Count Two, 07 CR 378, the crime of rape, the court orders you to serve a term of ten years in the Department of Rehabilitation and Corrections.

"Count Three, the crime of rape, the court orders you to serve a term of ten years in the Department of Rehabilitation and Corrections.

"Count Four merges with the rape offenses, and no sentence is imposed.

"Count Five in 07 CR 378, gross sexual imposition of Torey Votaw, the court sentences you to 18 months in the Department of Corrections. The sentences in those particular—in that particular case are ordered to be served consecutive to one another.

"Case 07 CR 1262, gross sexual imposition of █████ █████, the court orders you to a sentence of 18 months in the penitentiary.

"Case 07 CR 1262, the rape of █████████, the court orders you to a sentence of ten years in the penitentiary.

"Those sentences are ordered to be served consecutively to one another and consecutively to the sentences in 07 CR 378.

"While in the penitentiary, you are not to ingest or be injected with any drugs. You are to submit to any testing requested by the department, and those tests are to indicate that you did not ingest nor were you injected with any drugs of abuse.

"Upon your release from the penitentiary, you are required to serve five years of post-release control subject to the rules of the Adult Parole Authority.

"If you violate their rules, they can add more rules, or increase the time you are under supervision, or they can take you back to the penitentiary for up to nine months each time you violate..."

There's that word again: violate. I felt nauseous again. I was violated. Samantha was violated. And unfortunately, so were these other women.

"...and they can accumulate those periods to add up to one-half your total sentence.

"If you violate the law while on post-release control, then in addition to the prosecution and punishment for the new crime, or even instead of it, you will be taken back to the penitentiary on these crimes again and then ordered to serve the greater of whatever is left on the five-year period of supervision or one year.

"From these sentences you have the right to appeal. This court will appoint counsel and provide all papers and documents necessary for your appeal at the state expense if you are unable to afford those things. You have 30 days from today's date to perfect an appeal by filing a notice in the Seventh District Court of Appeals. Anything further from the State?"

"No, Your Honor, thank you," Natasha said.

"Anything further from the Defense?" the judge asked.

"No, Your Honor."

It's done. We did it.

I squeezed Samantha's hand as well as the woman next to me. My heart was racing and though there was a huge sense of relief, it was somewhat surreal that it was all really over.

He's going to prison for forty-three years.

Forty-three years.

Amazing. I don't think I have ever truly felt this soul deep gratitude. Why didn't he just own it and take the plea?

Forty-three years.

So many people had helped us to understand what all those charges meant and what everything translated to for us. So many people stood behind us, if not physically, we knew they were there in spirit. They supported what we were doing and why it was important. All the people in the victim witness office and the bailiffs were amazing. They showed true care and concern, and even had the ability to make us laugh once in a while. This was not an experience I would wish upon anyone, but justice was served. We could move on, knowing he wasn't hurting anyone else (at least not outside of prison) and maybe it all was kind of a big deal.

Chapter Twenty:
Happiness at Home

Summer 2013

I smiled to myself as I mixed the seven-minute frosting for
her cake. An electric mixer will forever remind me of my Grandma
making this frosting for my Grandpa and this recipe especially was
a long-time family favorite. The first time she'd eat straight up
SUGAR would be Grandpa cake (though it would be gluten-free).
*I can't believe my baby girl is one, and my little boy is
three! What an amazing life we have.*
I was in the very small and not awesome kitchen of my
dream home, getting ready for our daughter's birthday, while Jay
played with the kids in our pool. We'd bought this little 1940's
bungalow with coved ceilings, hardwood floors, and a fantastic
pool not long after we got married four years earlier.
I stopped the mixer and licked a beater.
Yum.
I added just one drop of red food coloring to make the
frosting pink, her favorite color, and gently pulled the cake out of
the pan. Smiling, I added a single cupcake to the top.
This will look like her binky, and she LOVES her binky.
I giggled to myself at the thought of her round cheeks and
exuberant spirit. She was a total joy of a baby, and now she was
already an independent and spunky little toddler. With her bright
eyes and her mischievous smile, Emi G. was a fire cracker.
My kids are amazing. I'm so lucky.

As I slathered the pink frosting on the chocolate cake, Jay came bursting through the door from the backyard with a towel around him.

"We need snacks." He leaned over my shoulder to look at the cake and kissed my cheek. "What is it?"

"Her binky, of course. Is there anything she loves more?" I didn't try to hide the sarcasm.

"Ha! Perfect." He laughed as he opened the fridge. He was moving fast like he always did, as if getting snacks had a fast-approaching deadline just like work.

"There are bananas, grapes, and seaweed you can take out to them," I said as I watched this amazingly beautiful, tan, muscular man rummage around to get food for OUR kids.

Wow—four years! This good life is moving really fast.

"Her friends are going to be here pretty soon. Is the backyard ready?" I asked.

"I think so. What else needs to be done?" Jay asked as he juggled grapes, bananas, crackers, and cheese.

"Let's just take her highchair out so that she can eat her cake from there. How was swimming?"

"Great! Otis is diving under the water a lot now. He's a really good swimmer for three." Jay's voice oozed with pride.

"Yeah, O is swimming well and Em has NO FEAR. You've got to really watch her," I said as the image of her underwater flashed through my brain.

Ugh. I'm glad we got that fence installed.

He glanced over my shoulder again with the tray of snacks in his hands. "Looks good! Are you coming out?"

"Yes. I'll be there as soon as this is done." I nodded at him.

"Cool. I love this. Pool parties are awesome!" Jay exclaimed as he walked out the back door and kicked it closed with his foot.

I gently covered the cupcake with another swipe of frosting on the top and tried to clean up any and all little chocolate crumbs that I saw. Taking a step back, I grinned.

It looks just like a binky, and, it's is going to be destroyed by her in about five minutes. Ha!

I walked through the dining room and down the hall to our bedroom to change into a bathing suit. In my closet, I saw the box of wedding cards up on the shelf and beamed at the memory of that amazing day in Ohio on the shore of Lake Erie, promising to love Jay forever. We had both wanted kids and I was pregnant with Otis just a few months after we got married. Jay loved my big pregnant belly and didn't mind that my body had changed, or that I was no longer the rock-hard climber girl with whom he had fallen in love. He also never ran away from the relationship challenges that arise when one person has experienced any sort of abuse, let alone sexual violation. Jay had been the constant open and safe space I needed to continue healing on all the levels of my being.

I opened the French doors from our bedroom and walked into our oasis of a backyard. The kids were sitting on towels on the concrete patio eating their snacks, and they both looked up at me.

"Momma!" Otis shouted.

"Emi-bear" stood up and toddled over to me. I picked her up and snuggled her wet bathing-suited self as she gave me a big hug, while Otis continued to devour his grapes.

"Happy birthday, my love!" I said as I gave her a squeeze and kissed her soft chubby little cheeks.

"Momma," she said with a big drooly smile and leaned her head against me.

Mmmmm. I love this kid. I love being a mom. I just can't get enough of my baby girl.

I plopped Em down on her towel and walked through the yard, tossing toys into the sandbox. Jay was sitting in a chair, laying back with his eyes closed, drinking in the Central Valley sun. I looked at my amazing little family.

Life is so good.

My mind raced back through memories of my children's lives. There was the incredibly empowering natural birth with Emi, and then a week later, on Otis' second birthday, we were back in the hospital with her because she had a fever. The year before that, I'd had a miscarriage right before Otis' first birthday. And then, I shuddered when I thought back to Otis' birth and his week in the

NICU.

I hope this year's birthdays are a little less stressful. We deserve to have a happy and fun few birthdays!

Just then, Brutus ran to greet our friends! Melissa and Allison and their families came pouring through the gate.

"Happy Birthday, Emi!" They all yelled, almost in unison.

"Can we swim?" Melissa's daughter asked with anticipation in her voice and eyes.

Melissa smiled as she dropped her bag of towels on a chair. "Sure! Let's swim for a bit and then we'll have lunch."

The husbands collected at the table and Jay offered beers, which were happily accepted.

"Otis, Em, do you want to swim with your friends?" I asked.

"Yes!" Otis replied and was quickly through the gate and jumping in the pool. Em toddled over to me and reached for me to pick her up.

"You want to swim with Momma?" I asked, and she smiled and nodded.

Awesome. It's hot and I'm ready to play in the pool for a while too. I can't believe this is my life and these are my friends.

The crew of moms were all in the pool and there were six kids from one to seven years of age all swimming too. It was great. All the kids but Emi could swim, so the three of us moms all gathered in a corner where we could stand and let Em try to swim back and forth between us.

"She is such a water baby. She loves it!" Melissa smiled as she reached for her.

"I know! I think she'll be a swimmer next summer for sure," I said, proud of my fearless little girl.

"I can't believe she's a year old already. Seems like a week ago that you were pregnant with her." Allison glanced around at the kids, giving words to what we all were thinking.

They grow up so fast.

We swam and played for an hour or so and then the kids started getting hungry.

"Should we do lunch and cake? Em's going to need to go

down for her nap in about an hour." I looked at the other moms as I climbed out of the pool with her.

"Sure. I'll unpack our picnic and get the kids out of the pool," Melissa said, and started moving towards the steps herself.

I wrapped Em in a towel and carried her into the house to get her changed and dry. As we walked through my bedroom she snuggled up against me and squeezed. She was such a little snuggler.

Mmm. It's good to be a mom.

I dried her off and she pointed to her birthday hat/tiara.

"Hut."

I dried her head with the towel, kissed her sweet little cheek, and placed the white feathery hat on her head.

"How's that?"

She smiled her mostly toothless grin at me and patted the hat.

"Gentle," I said, hoping she could make it through the cake eating without destroying the sweet gift given to her by one of my medical assistants.

She doesn't really need clothes, I thought, as I picked out my favorite pink cloth diaper for her.

"Pink?" I asked as she laid back on the changing table knowing the drill. She reached above the table to the little box that held her binky, grabbed it, and popped it in her mouth.

That's my Emi.

The rest of the clan was outside snacking on lunch and I took just a few quiet moments inside with my baby girl.

"Want to go eat your cake, Shnookums?" I asked, knowing we had a short window before she was going to crash out for a nap. She reached up for me and I picked her up to carry her out to her party.

Jay had her chair set up for her and all the other kids were devouring their veggies and meat rolls in anticipation of birthday cake to come.

"Can I help Emi open her presents?" Melissa's daughter asked as she brought a purple bag with pink paper over to Em's chair.

"Sure." I smiled at her sweet six-year-old mothering. "But, let's do cake first. Are you ready?" I asked.

"Yes!!" It was a loud chorus from all the kids. Jay and I went inside to grab the plates, forks, and the binky cake. It felt cool inside the house.

"Central Valley heat is cranking up already. Can you believe our baby is one? Time is flying." I hugged him tight from behind and kissed his warm, sun-drenched shoulder. He turned around and pulled me in to a face-to-face hug.

"It is. I love our little family. I love you and your binky birthday cake," he said, squeezing me tight.

"Thanks, hon. Let's get this stuff out there before she falls asleep in her chair."

I put the final touch on the cake, a single candle, and carried it outside. Jay followed with the other cake for the rest of us. The kids all flocked around us to look at the cakes, and childhood excitement pulsed in the air.

Em looked up at me and clapped her hands, the white feathery birthday hat still in place. I put the binky cake in front of her and started singing, "Happy Birthday to you," as all the kids joined in the song. Otis was right next to her chair, but didn't even stick his finger in the icing. He was watching his baby sister with a bit of jealousy and a lot of love.

As the song finished, she looked at the cake in front of her.

"Try it, Em." I encouraged her. She looked up at me, not sure what this thing was. Then, she tentatively touched the frosting. It was soft, it felt good. She licked her hand, and her eyes lit up and she smiled. She grabbed a bigger handful of icing and put most of it in her mouth, but a lot on her face. She squeezed the icing in her hand and then grabbed more with her left hand. This was fun!

Otis stood patiently next to her. "Get to the cake, Emi," he said with a wisdom that only a three-year-old possesses. She looked over at her brother and held her icing filled hand out to him. He took a lick and she smiled. It was just like when she fed the dog from her high chair! She giggled as Otis licked the icing from her fingers and all the kids were laughing.

This is it. We've made it. Life is good.

Chapter Twenty-One:
Triggered in the Tropics

April 2015

Benjamin, our teacher, put his hands out and mimicked his gymnastics coach lifting him to the high bar. That simple movement triggered my heart rate to increase and I lost the words that he was speaking.

Suddenly, I could feel Greg's hands on my waist. My mind started racing through the last few weeks' events, and I was gone from the amazing retreat I was attending in Costa Rica.

Why does this shit still get me so worked up? I should be here in this amazing moment!

I was sitting in a sunny tropical classroom (or yoga studio) with 35 other souls for the start of a personal and business development retreat, but my mind went back to the city park in California just a week before.

My friends Melissa, Allison, and I were hanging out on our Tuesday morning playdate. I was the last to arrive and began laying out my blanket and unpacking my snacks and water.

Melissa spoke first. "Torey, did you hear about Carl?"

I could tell by her concerned tone of voice, it wasn't anything good.

"No, what's up with him?" I asked, thinking maybe he was sick or something happened to him.

"He was arrested last night on a bunch of counts of molestation of young girls," she reported with a grimace.

"Oh my God. Seriously?" My stomach dropped. That was not what I was expecting. This guy had been the worship leader at our church for the past year.

It took a lot of time and acceptance for me to go back to an organized church and now this, at a place I have started to trust?

My heart started beating faster, and I felt just slightly nauseated. I knew that the details didn't really matter, but I also knew that I needed to talk through this stuff to process it.

"What else do you know?"

"There are videos, and multiple victims. That's really all we know right now. The girls were all music students of his and used to go to his house for lessons," Melissa said with heartfelt sadness.

Allison looked at me with concern, and I could tell that she could see I was going into a downward spiral.

"He's thirty, right?" I asked, my voice beginning to waver.

"Yeah, I think so," Melissa said quietly.

"Ugh, that's exactly how old my gymnastics coach was. Isn't it amazing that we didn't know? I mean, we all know Carl; you guys better than me, but I see him most weeks. I never thought I wanted to hang out with him or anything, but had you asked me last week if he was molesting kids, I don't think I would have said "Yes." This is what terrifies me! They are so hard to spot. This is why I'll never have a male babysitter for my kids." I could feel my heart rate escalating and could hear the anger in my voice.

"Torey, I'm sorry. I know this hits close to home for you." Allison's sincerity matched the sweet expression on her face.

"Thanks, I'm okay. It just brings stuff up for me. I can't help but think about those girls. It's so hard when you are young to know what love is anyway; and when you trust an adult and they start grooming you to do things that you know are wrong, it makes it hard to trust yourself, let alone anyone else. I wish I could talk to them."

"I know some of them, and I know they are already getting help," Melissa said in her natural, loving way.

"That's great. I'm glad they are reaching out already, and I'm so glad they reported it. That takes guts, especially when they are so young. I wonder what would have happened if we had reported Greg when we were young, instead of walking around for fifteen years as if it was no big deal?" As I said it, the possibility of a different life flitted quickly in and out of my mind.

It all happened the way it was supposed to. No regrets.

I still felt sick for those girls and scared for my kids going out into this world.

What the hell? He was right there in front of me every week. My radar did not go off like I would have hoped. How will I ever know if someone is going to try to hurt my kids? I'm so thankful he was never with my kids.

The disruptive sound of a bird flying in the door brought me back to the classroom in Costa Rica. A woman from our group gently picked up the bird and released it outside and the interruption gave me a chance to get up and stretch a bit.

I need to get this shit out of my head so I can be more present.

Benjamin finished with the information he was presenting and then another staff member came up to teach us a tool called WOOP. The woman who developed WOOP is Gabrielle Oettingen and it stands for Wish Outcome Obstacle Plan. We broke up into small groups, and I was lucky enough to be in a group with one guy who I already knew I really liked, as well as a girl that I loved from her original statement to our group, so I felt comfortable going into the exercise.

"Okay, so we're all going to WOOP something now," the bubbly positive psychology expert said.

I sat with my group and stared at the journal in front of me. It's the one thing that seems to be holding me back right now, so why not wish it away? We were all in our own worlds writing and I hesitated, but then I put pen to paper. It was uncomfortable to even write, but I did.

I WISH I could tell Benjamin about the Greg and Carl shit so that I could get it out of my head.

The Outcome would be that I would be able to be more in the present moment knowing that the leader of the retreat knows the baggage I am carrying right now.

The Obstacle is that it's hard to just grab Benjamin and start telling him about my history of sexual violation.

My Plan is that I will walk with Benjamin to his next meetup and tell him about the Carl and Greg shit as briefly and concisely as possible.

Our instructor was walking around checking on the groups and then after a few more minutes she said, "Okay, now I'd like you to share your WOOP with your group."

Hehe, that rhymes. But, ugh, there's nothing funny about this WOOP. I guess I can do this.

We picked an order and each person started sharing. Most people used wishes about their businesses and things that were keeping them stuck, but one other person shared something personal that had her a little emotional. I went last, thinking I would be able to read it with no problem.

I've dealt with this shit. The guy is in prison. Carl didn't hurt me or my kids. I can say this. I just need to get it out there, and it will stop rattling around in my mind.

But as I started, I could feel the emotion welling up inside me.

"This WOOP was created because Benjamin and I share a common history of being gymnasts," I said with a deep breath. "And when he made that movement as if his coach was helping him to the high bar, it brought up a ton of shit in me." I was shaking just a little, and my emotions were right on the surface.

Oh no, I don't want to be that overly emotional girl I was in grade school.

"So, here goes: I 'wish' I could tell Benjamin about my

shitbag gymnastics coach who sexually abused my friend and me."
Tears were streaming down my face already.

What the hell!? Why is this still so RAW for me? I've dealt with this. Everyone in the group was present and holding an amazingly safe space for me. I felt the love, so I moved on.

Whew, deep breath.

"The 'outcome' would be that I'd be able to be more present in the moment, knowing that you all and Benjamin know what's coming up for me." I was tearful, but I got it out.

Deep breath. I can do this. I was feeling more powerful as I went along.

"The 'obstacle' is that it's not that easy or fun to grab Benjamin and tell him my sex abuse story. And the 'plan' is to just do it. I'll walk with him to the next meetup at the cantina and tell him why I am a basket case." Tears were streaming down my face. "Sorry, guys. I can't believe this is bringing up so much shit for me."

Marsha leaned over and gave me a big hug. "It's okay, Love. That's some heavy shit. Remind me later and I'll tell you my story too."

"Thanks. It's amazing how many people have these stories, right? Thankfully, my coach is in prison, which is why I thought this wouldn't be so raw for me; but some recent stuff with a worship leader at my church seems to have ripped the band aid off."

"Understandable. I think you should tell Benjamin. I think it will help you," Marsha said sincerely in her adorable British accent as she gave me a side hug and we stood up.

"Thanks. Yeah. I can do it. Especially since I just unloaded all that on you guys! Ha! Thanks so much for listening. Okay— I'm going for it. WOOP, here I come."

I walked to the door as Benjamin was walking out and just dived right into it. "Can I tell you a story on our way over?"

"Sure," he said in his totally approachable, guy-next-door kind of way. He was wearing pumas and a T-shirt and jeans.

"Okay, so I was a gymnast too, and when you made that

motion like you were a coach lifting someone to a high bar, it totally brought up a bunch of shit for me. My gymnastics coach was a pedophile; and fifteen years after he abused my friend and I, we went to the police and ended up in a week-long jury trial that put him in prison for forty-three years."

Whew. I said it, and my shit is still mostly together.

"Wow. Okay. So how can I help?" Benjamin asked.

He didn't stop or play the "I'm so sorry" card. He just asked, without any energy behind it, how he could help.

Awesome. Thank you, Benjamin.

I teared up as I plowed on while walking in the humidity along the lush tropical path. "I just needed you to know. That's the help—that you know the story and why I am so raw. Right before I left to come here, there was a guy at our church who was arrested on a bunch of counts of molestation and it seems to have really affected me. I felt like if you knew, I could get it out of my head and be more present."

"Well, thanks for telling me. I appreciate you sharing. You might want to talk to Rebecca too, as she may have some resources for you if you need more help."

"Thanks, Benjamin."

Thank you for not showing pity or telling me you are sorry. I kind of hate it when people say that shit.

Later that afternoon, I found myself in the classroom with Marsha and a few other women from our retreat. "Torey, do you want to hear my story?"

"Definitely. Tell me please!" I said. A handful of us spread out in a big wide-open classroom and, with the space they created at this retreat, it already felt like any topic was fair game. We were all picking up the seats and bolsters we had used for our last session and, as we were gathering and re-organizing, Marsha started her story with all her energy, humor, and British-ness.

"So, I was probably about twelve when I met this guy on the subway one day coming home. I was really developed at twelve. I wasn't some twiggy little stick thing. I had most of these already," she said as she looked down and gestured toward her voluptuous breasts. "He told me that he was an agent and he thought that I'd make an amazing model. Then he asked me to come to his house, so that he could shoot photos of me. I was twelve and I thought, *'shit yeah,'* you know?"

She was cracking me up, as was her accent. She was such a great storyteller, I could imagine myself there.

"So, he told me to come by his place the next day and gave me the address and a time on this little slip of paper in the subway... When I got there, he had me change into some weird shapeless fleece skirt and he said we should dance to get me loosened up for the photos. You know, so I wouldn't be so nervous or whatever. And so, I'm dancing with this guy, and it's totally awkward, but I want to be a model, right? What twelve-year-old girl doesn't want to be told she's beautiful and she should be in pictures? Next thing I know, his hands are in my underwear! I didn't know what to do, I just kept dancing and assumed this as an essential part of training to be a catwalk model. He asked me if my (totally fictitious) boyfriend ever touched me there, and I said 'No' and he said 'Ah, that's why you're not relaxed.' And I thought, well yeah, that's sound logic."

By this time, I am about to pee my pants laughing at her story telling and the infectious smile on her face as she is telling it, but she just kept going as I laughed.

"Then he acted like he was going to take some pictures; but he never did. What the hell, right? Later that week, I was telling my friend Shelley about it, and she thought I was off my rocker to go there again, so I called him and told him I wasn't coming back."

"So, wait, you're telling me you cancelled your appointment for sexual abuse?" I asked, laughing at the thought of her at a payphone for some reason.

"Yeah, I guess I did. Hilarious, right? But at twelve, what do we know?" She said it thoughtfully, reaching back to that twelve-year-old version of herself and feeling empathetic.

"Oh, I totally get it. I think it's amazing that you had the wherewithal to stop it when you were so young. That's why these bastards are so dangerous. They make you think it's all okay—that it's no big deal. I'm so glad my coach is in prison. I don't think he ever would have stopped. Actually, I really hoped he had, and then I hoped he would take the plea deal, but he just denied it all in court, which showed me just how messed up he really is."

"Wait, wait. Who's in prison?" Stacie, my new friend, who was almost exactly the same height as me, jumped in and asked. We saw eye-to-eye both figuratively and literally. She's also a clinician with an alternative slant and a history of gymnastics.

"My gymnastics coach," I said.

"Woah, I missed that story. Why is he in prison?" she asked.

"I can tell it again if you want?" I asked, and she nodded. "Basically, he was raping a friend of mine who was a year or so older than me, and then he kissed me when I was 15. When I was thirty, my friend and I went to the police and reported it. A year and a half after that, we went to trial, and now he's in prison on a forty-three-year sentence. Look at me, I'm getting better and better about telling this story! We're swapping sex abuse stories—anyone else want to join in?" I asked letting it lighten in my brain and my body.

"Are you really laughing about this?" Stacie, who was a yoga and talk therapist, asked with a bit of concern on her face.

"I guess I am. I think it's better to laugh than to cry. Something needs to change in our society. There are SO MANY stories out there like this and RARELY does anyone report it. Pedophiles are everywhere. The worship leader at my church was just arrested for similar crimes, which is why this is so in the forefront of my mind. I told Benjamin today, because I just can't think about anything else. The fact that it still bothers me pisses me off, because I thought I had some serious closure when he went to jail." It felt good to talk about it and to share it with other women who understood.

Stacie looked concerned. "Yeah, but that stuff doesn't go away, Torey. It sounds like you've done a lot of good work, but this new thing has triggered you again. Yoga therapy might really help. I've worked with a lot of sex abuse survivors," she said with heartfelt concern.

"Yeah, even just non-therapy yoga is great for me. I saw a counselor for a year or so when I was first addressing it; and all in all, I think you're right, the worship leader was a major trigger. You know, it's not about me anymore though—it's about my kids. I worry for them. I want them to be safe, but I don't want to never trust them with other adults. I want them to have fun, but I'm terrified when I consider letting them spend the night at someone else's house. Now that I have a little girl, it's even worse..."

I felt my body tighten at the thought of my Emi having something like this happen to her. The mood in the room had gone more somber. I didn't want to be the downer and I didn't want the conversation to be all about me, so I tried to change the subject. "Let's get out of here. We only have a few hours of free time. Anyone want to go in the pool?"

We dispersed, and I went to my room to change into my suit, noticing that I felt a huge weight lifted compared to earlier in the day.

God, I hate that I talked about this shit so much today, but I do feel better. Sometimes I guess I just need to talk it out. I'm glad I'm here. I didn't know this would be the topic I'd be ruminating on in Costa Rica, but in a lot of ways, it's a big part of my story and who I am. Maybe it's part of the reason I am a homeopath and decided to create a homeopathy-based business a few years ago. Maybe it's why I don't think that throwing drugs at people is a good way to treat them. Maybe I never would have met Jay and I wouldn't even be here searching for a "Good Life" if this hadn't happened. I won't ever let this define me, but maybe it's a place I need to work more in order to try to help make a change?

Chapter Twenty-Two:
Writing the Wrong

Summer 2017

As I put one foot in front of the other on the trail, and inhaled the misty cool air, I couldn't help but feel gratitude for where I was, who I was with, and what I was doing. It was Wednesday, my writing day, but Beth had invited me to hike a fourteener and I only had one chapter left to write.

The book had been an amazing project thus far, and the fact that I had actually completed almost the whole manuscript in just over two months was incredible, but it wasn't easy. My body had taken on the tension I used to feel as a teenager. I even had back pain like I used to in high school. It took a bit of a toll, but at the same time, I felt the layers of the pain peeling away, and I came to revelations I never could have imagined if I hadn't taken myself back into those days many moons before.

Hiking was the best way to clear my mind and figure out what needed to be written, so I opted to hike first, then write. Unfortunately, the weather looked gnarly, and we weren't up for a sufferfest at 14,000 feet. We opted for an early morning hike up Herman Gulch, which was closer, shorter, and safer.

Win, win, win, because I didn't get my eight hours of sleep last night, as I was out with Jay at a concert at Red Rocks. I'm tired but can't imagine not being here.

"How have things been?" I asked as we navigated the roots

along the forested trail. I could smell the pine and feel the cool breeze on my cheeks.

Wow, I love it out here.

"Good, all in all. Chad is stressed out, and he tends to become a homebody when that happens, which is the opposite of what I want him to do right now. It makes it hard because I want to take the kids and do fun stuff, but he doesn't want to join us, and that's not my point in leaving him at home. I want him with us." I could hear a slight strain in her voice. Chad had been really sick recently and it wasn't easy on the family. Beth and Chad had a son Otis' age and a daughter Emi's age and so our families had spent some time playing and camping together. All the kids and the adults got along, making them a rare and special find.

"I bet that's hard. I know he's got a lot on his plate, but I hear you on wanting to get out and live life, especially when you've all been thinking about the gravity of his situation. It always makes me feel more grounded and in control when I get some time away from home, just playing in the mountains." As I said it, I realized this was the first hike I'd been on in a long time.

I need to heed my own advice.

We turned a corner on the trail and started north up the gulch. We could no longer hear I-70, the freeway that we started out near.

Ah, that's better, I thought as I found my pace and listened to Beth.

"Exactly. I want to get away to Crested Butte or somewhere remote and beautiful, just be together, just the four of us, but he's not up for it right now. I have to understand that." She said it with a bit of remorse, but also compassion.

I like the way she thinks and speaks.

"Yeah, I get it. It's got to be hard for him not knowing what comes next, and wanting to be strong for you and the kids, but also doing what he wants and what feels good to him too. Your husband is a good guy." As I said the words, I thought about how special it was to know a little about what goes on in someone else's house.

We don't always take the time to talk like this.

"I know. He is an awesome guy and I'm so glad I have him. It's been hard, but I think we are doing well, all things considered. You learn a lot about people when things get tough, don't you?" she asked.

"You do. And you have the conversations that are most important. This past year or two I feel like I've gotten a lot more intentional about how I live and the things that I want to do. Our summer got a little derailed and we didn't get to camp as much as I would have wanted, but I had the intention. We all get so busy and next thing you know, we have a soon-to-be second grader and a kindergartener! Crazy! I think Masterminding has helped me a lot with sticking to my intentions and planning both my business and my life."

"What's a mastermind?" Beth asked curiously.

"It's a small group of people, typically entrepreneurs, who meet regularly to share knowledge and resources and think deliberately. It's a powerful tool. I've had one for a few years now and I love facilitating them. Jay and I planned a ton before we took the year off in 2007 and we're already planning for our year on a boat in 2021. If you aren't intentionally planning an adventure like that, it'll never happen. I love vision boards for exactly that reason. Have you ever done a vision board?" I asked, thinking about how I love to dive into creative planning.

I'm such a self-development nerd now, I thought hearing what I had just said.

"I used to write down my goals, but never a true vision board," Beth said, as she paused to take in the magnificent views around us. "And when I stumble back on those goals that were written down, it's amazing, I've accomplished most of them."

I smiled. "Funny how that works, huh?" I appreciated the beauty around me as I walked.

Colorado! It's so good here.

We came up over a small ridge and could see the vast mountains on both sides of us now, with scattered patches of snow, and we could hear the raging creek below us. The meadows were covered with thousands of wildflowers of red, yellow, purple, blue, and white.

This is why I live here. This is what I love.

"Vision boards are fun. I'd love to do a couples one with Jay. Maybe we could get together and have a couple's vision boarding night?" I said excitedly.

I'm such a nerd. Who asks their friends over to vision board together?

"That sounds great. Let's do it. How about you—how's the book coming?" she asked.

"I sent the first nineteen chapters off to my coach earlier this week, and I was supposed to be writing the last chapter this morning, but this walk will be a good setup for clearing my head and making sure I write what needs to be written." I smiled as I said the words.

I wrote nineteen chapters. That's nuts!

"That's awesome. It seems like you did that fast. How do you feel about it?"

"You know, it's been hard, but my intent wasn't necessarily to just write all the details of my story; it was to put someone into my head and show them how I felt, so that if they could relate to any part of it, they might see some path toward healing. I just worry so much for our girls with people in positions of power who obviously do not respect women and convicted rapists who only spend three months in jail. How are we going to change this culture?" I asked, as the magnitude of what I was writing about and why I was writing it dropped into my heart like lead.

"Yeah, I don't know. But it seriously weighs on me every day. I can't stand the stuff going on right now. I'm glad that the stories are getting media attention, but it's becoming clear how many coaches, clergy, teachers, and others in power positions are using that to abuse young people." There was disgust in Beth's voice as she said it, and I think we both felt it in our guts.

Beth gets it. Thank goodness, I have people like Beth in my life.

"I don't know. There are so many examples of women who

have tried to report and been shut down, sometimes before they even get a chance to file a police report. Those who do can end up having to re-live the story for months or even years and then most times the punishment is fairly soft. I'm so grateful that our case ended the way it did. I still think a lot of the true healing came for me when I reported the crime, but I'm not sure that's the case for the other victims. Everyone has their own path on this kind of a journey, and no one thing is right. I wish more people took the time and space to heal, so that we could better protect the next generation and stop the cycle."

"How long did your coach get sentenced to?" Beth asked.

"Forty-three years," I said.

"What? Forty-three years. That's crazy! Is that normal?"

"I don't know. I doubt it. Sentencing laws and even sex crime laws are different state to state I think. We had a 'by the book' kind of judge and the span of the years between Greg's offenses showed that he was probably never going to stop. Who knows if the police ever even dug into the other places that he lived. There might be a whole lot more victims out there, but if they have enough evidence for a case, I think the state moves forward leaving some stones unturned. I hope if there are victims in the other places he lived, that they heard about it and saw the outcome. That might provide some degree of healing in and of itself." I was happy to be outside talking about this subject. Letting the words flow out of me and then giving them up to the mountain to take on.

It's hard to hold this all the time.

"That makes sense, I guess, but that still doesn't mean that anyone who rapes someone should only get a few months." Beth said it with fierceness and conviction.

"Agreed, I mean, it is a felony. I'm glad the current cases are getting so much publicity now. The women who are coming forward and reporting and even testifying are total heroines. As a victim looking to report, let alone prosecute, it's so easy to just give up. It took a year and a half from when we reported until the trial and all that time Samantha and I were living on high alert. It was rough, but thankfully she had married Brad, who was a friend of mine from college, and he was a total rock for her, just like Jay was for me."

As I said the words, I couldn't help but smile. The thought of Samantha and Brad still just made me giddy.

What better thing could come from our reunion than Samantha meeting her husband?

"She married your friend from college?" Beth asked with surprise.

"Yeah, there were a lot of divine interventions that happened in our story, the first of which was Brad and Samantha getting married. He was a good friend of mine through college, and he happened to be living in Ohio just twenty minutes from her when we reconnected. When I went back to Ohio to make the police report with Samantha, I introduced them, and they started running together. They were married within a year, and now they have two awesome kiddos, an incredible house in the woods, chickens, and a golden retriever. The good life!"

How funny that our new lives were almost as parallel as our old lives, yet both SO MUCH BETTER.

"That's so great. What else was divine?" Beth asked brightly.

"Wow, there was a lot. Well, I was in Ohio because my dad was sick when Greg got arrested. That felt a bit surreal, but it was good because Samantha and I were together. And, get this, Samantha's birthday is March 10, 1975, and the statute of limitations in Ohio was 10 years if you were born on March 9, 1975 or before, but it changed to twenty years if you were born on March 10, 1975; so if she had been born a day before, we probably wouldn't have had a case. If that's not divine intervention, I don't know what is."

I'm so grateful that Samantha was willing to go to the police with me. If not for her, I don't think Greg would have gone to jail.

"That is crazy!" Beth said and then pointed to the ground around us. "Torey, are you seeing these flowers? This place is so beautiful. I can't believe we are so close to I-70. It's just magical out here."

"I know! I keep taking pictures of the flowers and the mountains and the clouds. It's actually great that it's trying to rain because otherwise I bet it'd be a scorcher."

"Agreed. This would be a great hike for the kids. We should get them up here soon," Beth said with a smile.

I loved that she was so game for adventures and seconded her thoughts. "Yes, we should. They could do this; it might take them all day, but they'd do it. And if it was hot out, they could play in the stream and the lake. I wish we had more time, summer is almost over. We're going to have all our kids at the same school this year, though, and that's going to be fantastic. One drop-off and one pick-up simplifies a momma's life!" I said with a sigh of relief.

"You can say that again."

We finished the two and half mile hike up, and landed at a stunning alpine lake just as the temperature started to drop and the wind kicked up. I spotted a large flat rock that looked like a great place to picnic and continue our chat.

I could talk to Beth all day, I thought, as I made my way to the boulder. Beth was a girl who could hang with the boys on her bike, just like I was a girl who could hang with the boys on my skis. We had the tomboy-athlete thing in common and the late-in-life mom thing too. We both had husbands and families we adored. But, as with all things, it might look different on the outside than the inside. We knew we weren't perfect and could sort through things while venting to one another without shame, guilt, or judgment. She was one of just a few friends in Colorado who I was close enough with to share the bad as well as the good, and I trusted that she could hold that space for me.

"So, when's the book going to be done?" she asked.

"Today I hope," I said laughing a little. "No, I'm not sure yet. I'm hoping to send the last chapter off to my coach today if I can get it written. It's been tough, but the hardest part is done, so I'm hoping we can wrap it up no later than the end of the year. My goal was to get the first draft done and edited by my birthday, and that's next Monday, so I think I got it. I'm looking forward to running more retreats and Masterminds to help people see what their healing journey looks like, and how I can help them facilitate that path. I also really want to collaborate with some powerful ladies and build a solid interactive prevention workshop for kids and parents. It's going to be good. I can see that my prior careers have all been leading to this, so I feel like I'm on the right track. And there have been some epiphanies for sure. I still held a lot of anger toward Greg last year when I started writing, and through this process I got to the point where I let it go. I'm not thankful that it happened, but I do think my life wouldn't be this awesome if it hadn't. I think it sent me on a quest for happiness which led to lots of rock climbing, skiing, yoga, and travel. When I see people who haven't dealt with an issue like this, they are not nearly as happy as I am. I am extremely grateful for my happiness. Whatever it is that I have in me that led me to take this journey, I am so glad I have it." I felt it in my heart as I spoke the words.

I'm glad my journey looks like this.

"Yeah, that's great, and it's a big deal. I wish that this wasn't so prevalent, and I'm glad you are trying to do something about it. The internet just brings a whole new set of craziness into our kids' lives too. What's it even going to look like in 10 years when they are looking at colleges?" Beth asked, reading my mind.

"I have no idea. I'm just hoping our little tribe of outdoor enthusiast parents can instill some good values in them and teach them they shouldn't live on the internet. I hope that we all stay happily married, and I hope that by the time my kids reach the age of fifteen, I'll be able to talk to them about this story in a way that isn't scary for them or triggering for me. If we can talk openly to our kids about sex without shame, judgment, or guilt, we'll be on the right path." I said the words hoping in my heart I was a strong enough mom to make it happen.

"That sounds about right," Beth nodded in agreement.

"It's all about them at this point, right? I mean, even our relationships with our husbands is so important to them. The health of our marriages is just vital. I want my kids to grow up knowing that two people can love each other forever—not that it's easy, but it's possible. It can even be fun if you like the person. I'm glad that Jay and I like each other so much. We can be jerks to each other when we disagree or are stressed, but all in all, we love each other no matter what. And I hope that alone will be really good for our kids. I also just took this self-defense class that has totally changed my perspective. It's got me thinking a lot on the skills I can teach my kids, and also a lot about consent."

We were heading back down from the lake now, taking in the natural beauty and just quietly enjoying. We hiked at a similar pace and both of us were comfortable in the silence. My mind wouldn't stop.

What do I want people to get from this book? How am I going to make a bigger impact? What can I teach my children about sex that would counter all the messages they see on television and in advertising? I mean, if I teach them to ask before they pet someone's dog, I should probably teach them to ask before they kiss someone, right? Maybe that's it. Maybe part of the solution is teaching our kids to get verbal consent before they hug someone, kiss someone, or (GASP!) have sex. I can't even imagine that. When I was growing up, it was common to hear guys ask, "How far'd ya get?" That's not how I want my kids to talk or to think.

So many thoughts were rattling around in my head, and I just couldn't shake the topic from my brain. I stopped for a second, took a deep breath and looked up, and then spun to get the whole three hundred and sixty degrees of beauty.

I'm on the right track. As hard as this has been, I feel like I am moving in the right direction. Everything about where I have been and where I am going seems to fit right now. There's an energy about this process that I've never felt before. I might not be able to stop childhood sexual violation, but at least I can open space to talk about it openly and hopefully make a change for the better in this society.

Beth and I made the turn that allowed us to hear I-70 again and we passed a few people on their way up. We scampered down the trail, happy we weren't on the top of a fourteener with raging winds and hail.

At this rate, we'll be back in town at 10 a.m. with plenty of time for me to write my last chapter.

"What are you up to for the rest of the day?' I asked Beth.

"Not too much since I was planning to hike most of the day. What about you?" She asked with a raised brow.

"I'd love to go grab a cup of tea with you, and then I'm going to go home and finish the book."

She smiled at me as we climbed into her car. "Sounds like a plan.

Epilogue

No Big Deal

Winter 2018

For most of my adult life, I held on to this story as "no big deal." While writing, I kept a running list of potential titles, and *No Big Deal* really stayed with me because it was the belief that held me back from addressing the truth for so long. Also, and very unfortunately, I believe it's the way our society views this behavior. However, that's just the tip of the iceberg. There's more to it than the secrecy and the minimizing; there's a social acceptance of it. In other words, I think that the words "No Big Deal" tell my old story, but it doesn't capture my new one or the one I'm determined to co-write for our culture.

If you've read my story, you know more about me than some of my close friends. You've seen a window into my inner world, and I am honored that you took the time. I could never share what you now know on a stage in twenty minutes, but that doesn't matter. The bigger message isn't about my story... it's about all the stories out there.

This story was told as honestly as possible, from my perspective at the time each moment happened. While writing, I was able to get back into the head of my fifteen-year-old self, and to think and feel the way she did. I went back to the days of frustration, shame, and guilt around my coping habits, though I didn't even know that's what they were at the time. I felt love and shed tears for Greg. I wondered about and hoped for the well-being of his family. I was able to re-live the outcome of the trial without re-living each painful and eye-opening day. Through the writing, I have healed even more. I have felt gratitude for my story because, had I not been so low, I may never have climbed so high.

I feel honored to be able to speak about this topic and I feel motivated to do so because I know so many strong, complete, and beautiful people cannot. I am looking closer at our societal views on sexuality and I am worried for our future generations. I now have one simple new thought on how we can make things better—by opening space instead of stuffing it away.

If you care about this topic, I invite you to **Open Space for CHANGE**.

Open space for conversations, as uncomfortable as they are. We need to shed light on the reality of this situation so that more people are aware and empowered to take action.

Open space for healing for those affected by sexual trauma. You know someone who has a story like mine. Hold open space for them. Be a warm place for them to come to as they process this trauma. Hear them. Believe them. Ask them what they need.

Open space for prevention. I've participated in several programs that address prevention, but we need more.

If my story resonates with you and you want to be part of Open Space, reach out and join the movement. I am building a network of powerful people to bring more prevention into the world to help you and those you love, so please stay connected if that's a network and movement you want to join.

This type of change takes big conversations, many hearts, and a lot of open space.

www.openspace4.com

Acknowledgments

To my amazing rock of a husband, thank you for being you. Thank you for supporting me when the pain bubbled up and I may not have had the words for it. Thank you for allowing me the space to play in this entrepreneurial world even when it gets hard. Thank you for being so kind and patient from the moment we met. Thank you for not just believing in me but expecting great things from me. You are and forever will be my rock.

To my Otis, always creating, giggling, wriggling or running. Your fearless approach to the world shows me that I too can do anything. Thank you for helping me learn patience, forgiveness and self-control.

To my sweet Emi, always singing, dancing, snuggling and writing. What would I do without your joy, cheeks, and love? Thank you for showing me that if I just keep breathing, incredible things come out of me.

To my mom, dad, brother, Bob and my incredible family-in-laws. Thank you for loving me through this journey and believing me when I told each of you. I know this story has impacted you all. Hurt people hurt people, and typically it's those closest to them. I'm sorry for the hurt, and I love that you love me anyway.

To my gramma and grampa, you were my constant source of support and stability. Grampa, I couldn't speak these words when you were alive. Thank you for always being my biggest fan.

To "Samantha", thank you for standing by me and continuing to move forward when it got hard. Thanks for holding down the fort and allowing me to be me, while you continue to be you. We'll always have this, but now we have so much more.
To all the gymnasts mentioned in this book. I miss you. I miss what we had before this story turned ugly. I know that Greg hurt more than just Samantha and myself, and I hope that we can reconnect and heal together. It is my hope that we can turn any shame, guilt, pain or regret left into a movement to prevent abuse for future generations.

To Molly, you are truly my sister. Thank you for every minute you spend on the phone with me reflecting the good parts of who I am and what I do. I would not be me without you.

To Natasha, Heidi, Detectives Flara and Stepuk, and Judge Krichbaum, thank you for doing your jobs so well, you were all instrumental in the journey to justice.

To the Hot Mamas That Mastermind, thank you for trusting me and showing me what two to four hours a month with badass ladies can do for my heart and mind. I love you all very much, and I love us.

To Amanda Johnson, thank you for speaking my language. Your soft words, open heart and absolute genius made me comfortable enough to start this journey and strong enough to finish it. You helped me write "more me." From our first conversation, I knew I was keeping you in my life forever. Thank you for holding my hand (and space) through this entire process and gifting me Abby and Ursula in the process.

To Melissa and Bob, thank you for your editing skills. Melissa, thank you for using a fine-toothed comb and most importantly the word "hopeful" after reading it.

To my Facebook story group. Thank you all for cheering me on and giving feedback along the way. Thank you for witnessing the messiness of it all and keeping me strong.
To my Maple Grove Moms (and a few dads), our after-school hang outs have been essential. Your support, understanding and help with kids have saved me more than you know. Thank you for being my village.

To my GLP tribe, and especially my 2015 immersion buddies who were a huge catalyst for this book and movement. Thanks for continually putting more love into the world.

To the women I know who are already leading the way in prevention. Feather Berkhower of Parenting Safe Children, thank you for giving me tools and hope regarding prevention. Lisa Foster, her Parillume community, and her Voice and Choice CLub, thank you for shining so brightly in the world and showing me how beautifully it can be done. Amelia Dorn, IMPACT Personal Safety of Colorado and my BABs. Toes to the mat! Let's change this world.

To all my amazing male friends, and each of the men that I dated in the past. Thank you for letting me share some of your stories. I was fortunate to have each one of you in my life for a time. You taught me huge lessons. Thank you for loving me as I was.

To all the people who are mentioned in this book, thank you for allowing me to tell my story as true to life as I could, and more importantly, thank you for being a part of my life and my story.

Finally, I'd like to thank every person who has shared their story with me. It may have been in a doctor's office, at a climbing gym, after a leadership meeting, at a picnic table, on a bus ride, over email or social media, but you spoke your truth to me. For many of you, I am the first person you have ever shared that story with, and I am honored. Own your truth and open space for healing. You are complete, strong, and enough just as you are today.

About Torey

Torey Ivanic, founder of Open Space, is a Classical Homeopath, Mastermind Facilitator, and Author who helps people live authentic, intentional, healthy lives with purpose and connection. She's also a wife and mom who gets outside and plays in the Open Space as often as possible.

Her unique experience as a physician assistant and homeopath compelled her to seek justice and prevent further abuse at the hands of her perpetrator. Throughout her healing journey, Open Spaces have nourished and soothed her soul. Outdoor spaces such as mountains, oceans, or fields of flowers, and indoor spaces such as yoga studios, therapist's office, writing retreats, and self-development programs, have worked together to enable and empower Torey to heal her body, mind, and soul.

The message of this book changed as she finished writing it. She thought her goal was to write it for her thirty-year-old self and help people who needed to heal from a similar trauma and its inevitable collateral damage and relationshit. By the end, she knew she was also writing it for her children and future generations. She wants to be a part of the upstream change—not just healing for the wounded, but prevention through a grassroots movement to teach parents and children the tools and skills they need to stay safe and healthy.

She resides in Golden, Colorado with her partner in life, Jay; her inspiration for living better every day, Otis and Emi; and their dog, cat, and three chickens. Team Ivanic can be found adventuring in the Open Space on snow, rock, dirt, water, and ice whenever possible.

Made in the USA
San Bernardino, CA
17 July 2018